JUBAL'S RAID

BOOKS BY FRANK VANDIVER

PLOUGHSHARES INTO SWORDS: Josiah Gorgas and
  Confederate Ordnance (1952)
REBEL BRASS: The Confederate Command System (1956)
MIGHTY STONEWALL (1957)
JUBAL'S RAID (1960)

  With Others:
FIELDS OF GLORY (1960)

BOOKS EDITED BY FRANK VANDIVER

CIVIL WAR DIARY OF GENERAL JOSIAH GORGAS (1947)
CONFEDERATE BLOCKADE RUNNING THROUGH BERMUDA,
  1861–1865 (1947)
PROCEEDINGS OF THE CONGRESS
  OF THE CONFEDERATE STATES (Parts of
  First Congress and all of Second Congress,
  3 vols.) (1953–1959)
NARRATIVE OF MILITARY OPERATIONS,
  by Joseph E. Johnston (1959)
AUTOBIOGRAPHICAL SKETCH AND NARRATIVE,
  by Jubal A. Early (1960)

JUBAL'S RAID

GENERAL EARLY'S FAMOUS ATTACK
ON WASHINGTON IN 1864

———————— * ————————

FRANK E. VANDIVER

McGRAW–HILL BOOK COMPANY, INC.
New York   Toronto   London

JUBAL'S RAID

For
SUSIE

PREFACE

A NEW GENRE of Civil War books has become popular: the "day book." These day books generally treat of some small segment of time, some minor incident. Vast research is done to enable the authors to flesh out their narratives with a staggering number of details—the aim, of course, to make the incident, the fleeting moment far more memorable than it appears to be in its normal historical context. One day, even a few hours, can take on special immediacy when all the hectic minutiae are brought together and a reader can relive—or appear to be reliving—the event from moment to moment. This genre has on occasion wrenched the historical continuum rather sharply, and forced a little moment, an insignificant incident, into heroic mold in such a way as to reshape history. When this is done, the historian becomes propagandist or worse, and all else is sacrificed to the market.

Now some may level this criticism, and with substantial evidence, at my championing the cause of Jubal Early. Yet it seems to me that there are legitimate segments of history, often overlooked, which may be studied in detail. Some of these are so peculiarly separate and distinct that perspective it not warped by intensive study. In the field of the American Civil War are many such segments, and perhaps one of the most notable is General Jubal Anderson Early's raid on Washington in the summer of 1864.

Early's raid occurred because General Lee needed somehow to relieve pressure on Richmond after Grant had hammered his way from the wilderness through the gore of Cold Harbor. When Lee sent Early westward toward the Shenandoah, first to deal with a Federal raid against Confederate communications, then to move upon the enemy capital if possible and perhaps force Grant to reduce strength in front of Richmond, a whole new phase of military operations began. What happened in the Shenandoah Valley during the remainder of 1864 happened largely because Jubal did what he did. His entire campaign from June, 1864 to March, 1865, might well be studied as a sterling lesson in strategic diversion; one distinct part of this summer campaign, the raid on Washington, might also be studied as an example of what a small mobile force under energetic leadership can accomplish by swift marching and hard fighting. All of Early's activities in 1864 are of interest to the military student, but his operations against Washington have fascination beyond the purely technical.

When his guns opened against the fortification around the Federal capital he had carried the banner of the Southland closer to the enemy's heart than the Yankee's had yet penetrated the heart of the South. His achievements were even more spectacular than that: the extent to which he frightened the United States is generally unappreciated.

Of all those bewhiskered, girded, and uniformed men of the War generation who loom larger than life, none could match Jubal Early in individuality. A cussing maestro, a hard-fighting soldier, an acid conversationalist, a sharp wit, he was almost *sui generis;* around him clung little of the

chauvinism of his age, and in retrospect he comes from history
as a modern man with modern ideas. Lacking sentimentality,
he had little concern for the magnolia tradition of the South.
He fought because he believed in his state and in the rights
it ought to have, not because of some moss-laden memory of
a South that never was. He fought hard and he fought to the
end, and when he had been whipped more thoroughly than
almost any other Confederate general, he rejected the reunited
States. A dedicated rebel he stayed, the most unreconstructed
of them all. He remains a vivid figure; tobacco cud working
angrily when he thought of the Yankees, eye flashing when
he went to fight them, laughing merrily when he enjoyed a
juicy joke with a much-suffering staff.

Those he took with him to Washington were not all sympa-
thetic to his flamboyant style. His second in command, John
Breckinridge, former Vice President of the United States,
Kentucky gentleman, soldier of note, looked the refined product of the old South. He was a tall man whose iron-gray hair
suggested his approaching middle age. His light-gray eyes
were steady and honest. He was the best of his breed, repre-
sentative of a society dying on the battlefields. To Breckinridge, Early appeared the harbinger of the new order, and
though he appreciated Jubal's dauntless aggressiveness, he
could never be the caustic cynic that his Virginia friend so
obviously was. With Breckinridge sided John Brown Gordon,
a division commander in Early's corps. Gordon, a straight,
tall, thin, fierce-looking Georgian, fought with the tenacity of
a bulldog, but he cherished the grace of the Cavalier South.
Early's harsh comments, his unsparing barbs struck Gordon
as ungentlemanly; effective, maybe, but ungentlemanly. And
there were other officers under Jube who shared the disap-
proval of the men from Kentucky and Georgia. But the rank

and file of Early's corps, the Old Army of the Valley, trusted him almost as they had Stonewall Jackson, and that stands as recommendation supreme.

Against Jubal in the weeks of campaigning south of Washington, appeared some of the more hapless Union generals, and now and then some of the best. David Hunter, Franz Sigel, and Max Weber ranked at the bottom of a long list; Henry Halleck, Christopher Augur, Quincy Gillmore were among the mediocre. But one of the Union's generals did his cause an important service in the campaign, a service which makes him a minor hero of the story: Major General Lew Wallace, who was to become world-famous as the author of *Ben Hur*.

Lurking always in the background is Grant, and standing over the whole raid is the figure of President Lincoln, himself a participant. The cast is stellar, the plot almost incredible, the action swift. Jubal's raid is one of those minor episodes in history with drama, pathos, high comedy, grim sacrifice, hairbreadth escapes, and inexorable tragedy.

FRANK E. VANDIVER

Rice University
June, 1960

ACKNOWLEDGMENTS

MY THANKS go to many for assistance in making possible the research for *Jubal's Raid*. First I should like to express my gratitude to the Fondren Library of Rice University. The Fondren staff put up with many tedious interlibrary loan assignments, helped to order material which became available in the perennial used-book catalogues, and patiently assisted in countless checkings of sources. The Library of Congress Manuscripts Division was especially helpful in speedily processing the microfilming of the entire Jubal Early collection, and this proved a chore of large proportions. The National Archives yielded some vital material on the Department of Washington, and the staff of the Civil War branch was characteristically cooperative. Many university and public libraries assisted, and I wish to thank them all in a blanket statement of appreciation.

Professor T. Harry Williams, gadfly of the Civil War, contributed of his vast knowledge and enthusiasm, and patiently listened to accounts of another Rebel fiasco. I am always indebted to him and to his charming Stell. More so now than ever.

Professor Bell I. Wiley, Emory University, Atlanta, Ga., called my attention to the Lucius Chittenden manuscript narrative, cited in the later chapters. I am indeed obliged for the reference; the document proved one of the most interesting of those used.

My graduate assistant, Mr. Archie McDonald, worked long and hard at transcribing notes, checking bibliographies and was especially helpful in preparing a copy of portions of the Diary of Jedediah Hotchkiss. Mr. McDonald is engaged in preparing an edition of Hotchkiss' journal and was able to add much background material to the diary's narrative of Early's Raid.

Rice University's unique typing service made the final copy of the manuscript for the printer, for which I am most grateful.

My wife, Susie, customarily puts up with more about the Civil War than anyone should have to, and I have dedicated this volume to her as a small token of appreciation for service above and beyond. Besides, she likes Jubal Early.

F. E. V.

CONTENTS

TROUBLES COME IN THREES

THE MUD in the Chickahominy bottoms recalled the Peninsula Campaign of 1862, when Little Mac had made his bid for Richmond. But the similarity ended there. Now the grayclads who huddled behind long lines of trenches near Cold Harbor were hardened veterans; their leaders were seasoned by the fiercest battle conditions in American experience. The commanding general, the commander of the Army of Northern Virginia, now had world renown and the deathless faith of his men. There were not as many to put their hopes in Robert E. Lee as there had been a few months before, but even the gruelling test of fighting in the Wilderness and Spotsylvania had strengthened rather than damaged Marse Robert's luster in the eyes of the survivors. And this was as it should have been, for he had led them since June, 1862, through the Seven Days, through Second Manassas, Sharpsburg, Fredericksburg, Chancellorsville, Gettysburg to the Wilderness, and though they had been hard pressed in recent months, the taste of victory lingered strong. His men were a special breed. Hard marchers, fearsome fighters, emotional, they earned the lasting admiration of their enemies, and one Federal officer would

1

label them for history: "That incomparable infantry!" Most
of them by this time were ragged, unshod, thin, and hard.
They made do with the little the Confederacy could offer. They
fought often without adequate munitions, they endured when
endurance seemed beyond hope, and they fought for Robert
Lee. They were his own now; their cause was the man who led
them, and they died for him without whimper or regret. What
Marse Robert required of them they gave him; and when he
asked beyond human achievement, as at Gettysburg, they still
tried. When people referred to them as the Army of Northern
Virginia, they were quick to correct—they were Lee's Army.
In the name there was pride, and in the belonging there
was valor.

Against Lee and his stalwarts the strongest army in North
America had marched in May of 1864. The Army of the
Potomac, after years of mismanagement and defeat, had forged
its own *elan,* risen above its mediocre generals and become a
fighting force capable of contending with the Army of Northern
Virginia. And at long last President Lincoln had found a man
who could wield this army and the other armies of the Union
as a coordinated machine. Ulysses S. Grant was not the direct
commander of the army—George G. Meade, hero of Gettysburg, was—but Grant ran it and the Union's war. The boys in
blue now were in the hands of capable men; they came to the
ranks in swelling numbers, and they fought with a spirit and
certainty born of long experience and Yankee persistence.

This persistence gave Grant the sobriquet of "hammerer"
during the summer of 1864. He nudged Meade into an advance
in early May—an advance timed to coincide with a major push
by Sherman in North Georgia. These two thrusts were part of
Grant's plan to end the war. In effect, he had returned to
Winfield Scott's old idea of the "Anaconda"—a general offensive against the whole Confederacy which would prohibit the

shuttling of Confederate troops from one section of the South to another. Without the chance of concentration, undermanned Rebel armies would nowhere match the Federals in field strength. The result of this sound logistical strategy was the furious campaigning in Georgia—Dalton, Resaca, Alatoona, Adairsville, Cartersville, the Etowah, Kennesaw Mountain, Atlanta—and the blood baths in the old Chancellorsville country.

The awful carnage in the Wilderness throughout May shook the North. Casualty lists etched the pages of almost every Northern paper—the Wilderness, Spotsylvania, the Bloody Angle, Enon Church, all presented their butcher's bill. And instead of taking a licking and drawing back to reorganize, Grant called for more cannon fodder and moved by his left flank closer to Richmond. Each red mile brought the enemy capital nearer, but each inch cost the Union dearly. Some wondered at the madman, Grant. Lincoln seemed set on slaying the flower of the North, set on trusting a man who had—so whispers had it—a penchant for John Barleycorn. How many lives were to buy Southern sod; how many to lie in it forever?

The climax came on the third of June, 1864, in an indescribable sea of mud—at Cold Harbor in the most awful thirty minutes known to the Union Army. When Grant's frontal assault finally sputtered out, 7,000 bluecoats lay maimed or dead in the ooze. Only 1,500 Confederate casualties were counted. Grant would later lament the assault, confess that the advantage lay with the defenders, but the deed had been done. His shattered corps lay behind their works while the brass pondered the next move. Grant's plan, despite the grisly encounters, remained essentially unchanged and had begun to work. Pressure in Northern Virginia and simultaneously in the Deep South strained Confederate resources almost beyond capacity. Cold Harbor was a good example: Grant could afford the loss, could replace his men; Lee could not. The Army of the Potomac must continue hammering. There could be no denying however, that heroic Confederate defensive efforts demanded heroic offensive measures against them. While Meade's men rested from slaughter, Grant began to bring the massive numerical and material superiority of the North into the campaign.

It required no great military perception to see that Lee clung to his lines by will and wile. He had anticipated every Union move from the Wilderness to Cold Harbor, and as long as he was able to slip ahead of the bluecoats he was able to stay between them and Richmond. What if other Union forces were to threaten portions of Virginia—the grain-rich Shenandoah Valley, perhaps? Other threats would force Lee to detach to meet them or to chance a desperate battle against the superior strength of Meade's army. Where the bludgeon failed, strategy might succeed. As Grant calculated, strategy dictated diversion.

No one knew better than General Lee the curious plight of his army. If his men had battled valiantly on the Wilderness campaign, if they had exacted more than seven times their pounds of flesh, they had still scarcely held their own. Steadily they had been forced to maneuver rearward in order to cover Richmond. The Cold Harbor orgy had been but a temporary success and the future hinged on the next turn of Grant's strategy. If he attacked again, good. If, however, he should slide once again to the south, cross the James and proceed with the sound project of approaching Richmond from its more vulnerable underbelly, then the situation would become desperate.

The peninsula between the York and the James offered little advantage to Grant: McClellan had proved the impracticality of operating astride the Chickahominy on a front well covered by Rebel works. But south of the James the terrain presented real possibilities. Between the James and Appomattox Rivers lay another peninsula known as Bermuda Hundred Neck. During recent weeks General Pierre G. T. Beauregard had been playing a daring game of ruse with the inept Yankee general, Benjamin F. Butler, and had contrived the effective containment of Butler's force along a relatively narrow enclave in Bermuda Hundred. Here Beauregard had constructed a defensive line which he held with barely enough men. Should Butler be reinforced by the bulk of Meade's army, Beauregard would be swept aside and the southern approaches to the Confederate capital exposed. Lee, then, must guard against this turning movement while he maintained vigilance at Cold Harbor. Grant had sufficient men to threaten both parts of the line, and if he did that, Lee had too few to retain control of the entire front.

Lee faced the prospect of protracted lines without enthusiasm. He gave some thought to forcing a fight with the Army of the Potomac ere it had an opportunity to aid Butler, but the odds counted too heavily against the venture. One other possibility worried Lee. Should Grant move the Army of the Potomac across Butler's rear, then across the Appomattox, he could make a dash for Petersburg, cut the Southside Railroad, interdict Confederate communications with the Deep South and be in position to cut off retreat from Richmond. While Lee pondered the main tactical threat to the Richmond sector, he learned of two other threats building outside of the capital area.

Constituting part of Grant's over-all plan of moving on Richmond were two large, mobile expeditionary forces. Both were worrisome to Lee since they seemed carefully planned and coordinated. One of these roaming forces apparently was aimed at the Shenandoah Valley, the other at Lynchburg. In the Shenandoah, that vast and vital granary of Lee's Army, Confederate forces had enjoyed small successes earlier in the year, and in May had gained a signal victory over hapless General Franz Sigel at New Market. There General John C. Breckinridge, former vice-president of the United States and lifelong politician now turned soldier, had beaten the Federals with a small force including the gallant cadet corps of the Virginia Military Institute. For a brief time after New Market, so safe had seemed the Valley that Breckinridge received orders to bring his little command to Richmond. He left the Valley under the protection of some scattered Confederate cavalry units and arrived in the Richmond sector in time to take part in the Cold Harbor operations.

The vacuum left by Breckinridge's departure had given Grant a chance to arrange his second threat to Richmond. He put this threat in charge of a highly regarded officer, General David Hunter, who commanded a large raiding expedition of about 8,500 men. Hunter was to move southward on Staunton, the old Confederate base at the southern end of the Valley. From there, he might progress eastward to threaten Charlottesville and Gordonsville. Or he might strike southeastward for Lynchburg, a vital Confederate supply point. Until Hunter's full plans were developed, about all that Lee could do about him was to direct General William E. ("Grumble") Jones, commanding the scattered Rebel units in the Staunton area, to impede his progress as stubbornly as possible.

Jones reacted to his assignment with characteristic decision. Collecting a force of about 5,000, he marched down the Valley to intercept Hunter's advance in front of Staunton and met him at Piedmont on June 5, 1864. In the battle there Jones' force was wrecked and Grumble lost his life. The next day Staunton, long the bastion of the Valley, fell to the Yankees. To those who had marched with Stonewall Jackson, had held the mountain passes through 1863 with ragtag forces of cavalry and militia, the loss of Staunton must have seemed an omen of the evilest kind. A mystic invincibility had guarded the town; the Blue Ridge had covered its right, the frowning Alleghenies its left, and a thin gray line its front. Legion upon blue legion had rolled up the Valley pike, only to break and wash back before Staunton. Now it was gone.

Hunter could afford to slow down. Other Federal columns were converging on Staunton, and he waited to build up his force. His men were not idle; they were put to work wrecking Staunton's capacity to make future contributions to the Confederate war effort. After a few Confederate sick and wounded were paroled, Hunter's men did a workmanlike job of destroying the railroad station, a steam mill, a woolen factory, and an important foundry. A quartermaster shoe factory proved difficult to destroy completely but suffered considerable damage. The Virginia Central Railroad, almost as ill-favored by war as the Baltimore and Ohio, had miles of track twisted out of service east and west of Staunton. Private property escaped heavy destruction, but local merchants felt the hand of pillage—all dry goods stores were stripped and grocery stocks vanished.[1]

On June 8 General George Crook's infantry and General William W. Averell's cavalry joined Hunter at Staunton. He now counted a total of 18,000 men under his command and felt the time had come to proceed with Grant's program. Move, Grant had ordered, to join a large body of cavalry under Sheridan in the vicinity of Lynchburg—Sheridan constituted the third Union threat to Richmond. Then do all possible damage to the James River and Kanawha Canal. Grant spelled out his desires carefully, lest the vital objectives of the Shenandoah–Central Virginia diversion be misunderstood by his com-

manders in the field. Hunter's mission toward Lynchburg
counted largely in the plans of the General-in-Chief of the
Armies of the United States. "It would be of great value to us
to get possession of Lynchburg for a single day," Grant wrote,
for it ranked as one of Lee's principal supply bases. "Lose no
opportunity to destroy the canal," Grant pleaded, adding that
damage to the Virginia Central Railroad was of equal importance.

In addition to the damage which Hunter's raid might do,
Grant thought it could also pin down Confederate forces in
the Valley. Wreck and detain, then, were Hunter's watchwords.
With Crook and Averell on hand, it looked as though good
wrecking might be done; as for detaining Rebels, there weren't
many left in the Valley to detain. In front of Staunton, hanging
on the Federal fringes, were some 2,000 Rebs under General
John McCausland, and they were about all the organized Confederate troops in the theater.

But Hunter was going to do more detaining than he knew;
he was, in fact, going to achieve the best possible objective of
a diversion—the detachment of part of the enemy's main
strength to deal with him. News of Jones' debacle and death
at Piedmont, and of the loss of Staunton, forced an agonizing
decision in Richmond.

On every Confederate front there were just not enough men.
Lee's Army numbered about 49,000 men: attached to it for
Richmond's defense were about 9,000 under John Breckinridge, 7,900 under Beauregard, and 7,400 holding the perma-
nent defenses of the capital.[2] Outside of the Richmond sector were scratch units near Hunter's army, some isolated
bodies in southwestern Virginia, and the splendid partisan
regiment of John Mosby in that section of upper Virginia called
"Mosby's Confederacy." If all scattered Confederate units
in Virginia were counted, there might have been 80,000 men

available. Against them were not less than 130,000 Federals, 18,000 of them in the Shenandoah area.[3] Faced with numerical inferiority, Lee pondered how best to meet Hunter's threat.

How many could go from Richmond without jeopardizing the city? Lee carefully sifted the confused information coming from the Valley.[4] All of it was bad. In the wake of Jones' death and the loss of Staunton, Confederate troops were virtually helpless. Scattered and demoralized they watched the Federals and called for help. Lee kept a clear view of the main problem, and summed it up in a dispatch to President Jefferson Davis: "It is apparent that if Grant cannot be successfully resisted here we cannot hold the Valley.— If he is defeated it can be recovered.— But unless a sufficient force can be had in that country to restrain the movements of the enemy, he will do us great evil." [5] To lessen the evil and at the same time hold Richmond, Lee decided on a limited detachment of strength. Back to the Valley area he ordered General Breckinridge and told him to take along the remnants of his division.

This detachment would mean minimum loss to the Army of Northern Virginia—now about 2,100 muskets [6]—but might achieve maximum results in an area Breckinridge knew so well and in which he might collect some 9,000 men of all arms. On June 7, Breckinridge pulled out of the lines and headed for Lynchburg.

No sooner had this second threat to Richmond been met than Lee received word of the third. Obviously part of Grant's plan of diversion into Lee's supply country, this threat came in the persons of General Philip Sheridan and 9,000 troopers.[7] The day Breckinridge's infantry marched way from Lee's works, Sheridan's column departed from Meade's camps and began its march to wreak havoc and to link up with Hunter. Lee and Davis understood clearly the threat he posed: a large mounted force could do fearful damage to the communications of the Army of Northern Virginia, especially to the railroads. General Wade Hampton, now commanding Lee's cavalry, thought Sheridan would strike for the junction of the Virginia Central and Orange and Alexandria at Gordonsville or Charlottesville.[8] Go after Sheridan, Hampton was told, and he began his march by dawn of June 9.[9] Now most of Lee's cavalry had departed, along with Breckinridge's men. The principle of concentration had been strained almost beyond the breaking point. Should any other diversion develop, Lee probably could do nothing about it.

Fortunately for Lee's Army, Hampton's expedition soon bore encouraging fruit. His division and that of General Fitzhugh Lee moved rapidly via inner lines; their troopers thought happily that they were on another of the great Confederate raids, this time to Washington. But by the tenth they could see that their route led toward Gordonsville. At the end of a long, hot day's march [10] Hampton's men bivouacked in gorgeous Green Spring Valley, and Fitz Lee's troopers camped near Louisa Court House, eight miles to the east. In the early hours of the eleventh Hampton moved out to attack Sheridan near Trevilian Station and brought on one of the most confused fights in the annals of the Confederate cavalry. Raging up and down unknown roads, trying to guard the Virginia Central to their backs, gray troopers found themselves fighting in several directions and at last had the shattering experience of learning that Yankees had worked around behind them and plundered their wagons. Hampton looked for Lee, who tried to get into the fight but found his way to the battlefield intercepted by Federals and fought virtually a separate battle. Hampton and Lee contrived to recapture most of the wagons, but could not re-establish contact with each other during the night. Fortunately, by nightfall Sheridan's men, especially those under George Custer, were so used up that the Yankee commander seemed glad not to continue the contest.

The morning of the twelfth produced no encounters, but in the afternoon a Federal reconnaissance in force met fierce resistance and was repulsed. With that, Sheridan decided his ammunition supply had dwindled too low, that his rations were equally scant, and that he had best not continue his search for Hunter. He retreated toward the Army of the Potomac that night.[11] The happy news of Sheridan's retreat relieved pressure from one of the three threats against Lee, but Grant still hammered and word about Hunter suddenly became alarming. Apparently the threat he posed had not been eliminated by detaching Breckinridge.

Breckinridge, watchful as he advanced west of Charlottesville, had learned on the tenth that Hunter had made a move. Quitting Staunton, Hunter had put his army on several roads and marched south. In a dispatch to Richmond, Breckinridge confessed he could not tell what Hunter's objective was, but his route could lead either to Lexington or to the mountain passes leading toward Lynchburg. No matter what his objective, Breckinridge had not the men to stop him.

Here was the extra emergency—the one which might stretch Lee's lines too thin. The problem of Hunter now created a division of opinion in Richmond. General Braxton Bragg, a weak but obstinate man who had, as a field commander, induced much of the ill-luck befalling the Army of Tennessee, thought the Valley must be cleared of the enemy. Since Bragg had been lifted to the post of military adviser to the President, his views had some weight. But Davis deferred to Lee, the one general he regarded as militarily smarter than himself. Lee wanted to clear the Valley, but felt that to do so would require the detachment of at least a corps from his army, and a corps could scarcely be spared.[12]

While Richmond worried about him, Hunter moved southward. Crook and Averell, operating on his right, skirmished
with McCausland's 2,000 and shoved them steadily back.
McCausland reported constantly to Breckinridge, whom he
now knew to be commanding in the Valley area. None of his
reports were encouraging; apparently he was not able to hold
north of North River and was falling back on Lexington.

The town would have been hard to defend with a large
force; with a small one it could not be held. But McCausland
tried. An old Virginia Military Institute man, he had sallied
from Lexington on hearing of Hunter's advance with the
jaunty comment that "we'll have to whip 'em again," [13] but
now he had his back to the town and to his beloved Institute.
While the Yankees were still a safe distance away, he had
asked that classes suspend and that the cadets once again stand
to arms for the defense of Lexington, and very probably their
campus. The corps readily turned out and assisted in efforts
to move military supplies southward. With definite word from
McCausland that Hunter was coming, indeed was only twelve
miles distant on the tenth, some cadet sappers with turpentine-
soaked cotton torches made ready to fire the North River
bridge when the last of the Confederate rear guard crossed.

It was touch and go. All night of the tenth and eleventh the
cadets were on duty, the bridge burners alert. Before dawn on
the eleventh, pickets sighted McCausland's weary men "streaming down the hills across the river." [14] Behind them a scant
half mile came the Yankees. The last-ditch rear guard finally
backed over the ridge above the river, retiring as skirmishers
and hotly engaged. McCausland got his main body across and
deployed along the craggy banks to help the rear guard. Artillery in position, the Confederates blasted away at the approaching bluecoats and for a small moment held them up. The rear
guard rallied to the bridgehead and dashed across. Instantly

the sappers touched off bales of primed cotton and the span disappeared in a pall of black smoke.[15]

Everything seemed to slacken, and a slow-motion drama unraveled in full view of observers atop the VMI plateau overlooking the river. A Federal battery came up smartly, unlimbered on the north bank and began firing. Shells arched over the river and fell around the Institute. The gunners were aiming at the towers, and great chunks of masonry and flying bricks filled the air. The cadet corps stood at parade in front of the main building, ready to brave the fire until ordered otherwise. While they waited, a Confederate battery replied from a position on the edge of the drill field. Finally came a heartbreaking order: move out. The cadets filed past the crumbling buildings and marched down the road leading southward. About five miles out of the town the column topped a ridge and turned to take a last look: the sight was one which many of the boys wished they had missed—"the day was bright and clear, and we saw the towers and turrets of the barracks, mess hall, and professors' houses in full blaze, sending up great masses of flame and smoke." [16] Behind the retiring cadets came McCausland's artillery and his broken horsemen. Finally the encouraging pop-popping of rear-guard fire faded, and all knew that Lexington was lost to the enemy.

Hunter's occupation of Lexington burned into the memory of Virginians. While some of his subordinates expressed revulsion at the wanton destruction of VMI, the damage done to several private homes, and the plunder of the Washington College Library, Hunter indulged his destructive proclivities.[17] Sacking the town occupied most of the twelfth and thirteenth, forty-eight invaluable hours.[18]

East of the Blue Ridge, Confederate brigadier John Imboden had been observing Hunter's progress and had kept Breckinridge more fully informed than had hard-pressed McCausland.

Breckinridge received with mixed emotions the news that
Hunter departed southward from Lexington on June 14. At
least the enemy would not approach Charlottesville or
Gordonsville, so two vital rail towns were safe. But his passage
south probably meant that Hunter was seeking a crossing of
the James River and perhaps a route directly to Lynchburg
from the west. Even if all Confederate units east of the Blue
Ridge, and those west which could get across, concentrated on
defending Lynchburg, the total Confederate strength would
probably not be adequate to deal with Hunter. But Breckinridge left the worrying to the high command in Richmond and
worked desperately to get a clear picture of where Hunter was,
what he was doing and as much intelligence as possible about
his intentions.

Hunter's intentions were pretty much as Breckenridge expected: to move via Buchanan, cross the Blue Ridge at the
Peaks of Otter and strike dead east for Lynchburg. After wrest-
ing that city from feeble defenders, he intended to wreck the
canal as Grant desired and then perhaps, in combination with
Sheridan, move south and rejoin the Army of the Potomac
below Petersburg. Such a raid would involve a great ride
around Lee and would assuage slightly the sting of Jeb Stuart's
two dauntless "rides around McClellan."

While Hunter plotted his campaign, Lee and Davis plotted
his destruction. The Army of Northern Virginia could ill
afford further detachment to the Valley area. Grant's operations continued around Richmond. Following the Battle of
Cold Harbor he had sidled once more to the left and had
briefly gone from Lee's glimpse while he crossed the James
and prepared to approach Richmond from the South. Below
the river, the Army of the James, under General Ben Butler,
still floundered in Beauregard's bottleneck at Bermuda Hundred, and Grant decided to cross behind Butler's lines there

and throw the bulk of his army against the ill-prepared works circling the southeastern approaches to Petersburg. In all the maneuvering around Richmond, Lee had to keep a screening force near the capital's defenses and sufficient strength in the field to hit any exposed portion of Grant's Army.[19] The theater of operations stretched almost thirty miles, and was cut by two major rivers, several lesser streams, swamps and unmapped bogs. Grant's strength of almost 120,000 men made possible intricate and extensive shiftings while Lee's numerical inferiority made him cautious.

Now, however, Lee had to face a decision which well could be the most audacious of his career. Bragg, Davis, Secretary of War James Seddon, everyone left the decision squarely up to Lee: what would be done about Hunter?

Anything done about Hunter meant jeopardy to Richmond. Jeopardy seemed a normal state in Richmond by now. The loss of the Confederacy's capital remained a remote yet horrid possibility. Richmond, like Washington, stood near the front, and, during McClellan's abortive Peninsula Campaign in 1862, the city had almost been the front. Citizens had grown used to the roar of cannon in the suburbs, to the tocsin sounding in the night, to alarms and rumors and fear in good measure. But always Lee's Army had stood fast, and the enemy had been thrown back.

Any Richmonder could have described in detail the importance of his town to the Confederate cause. Down by the James River stood the flaming furnaces of the Tredegar Iron Works, just about the only heavy-machinery plant in the entire Confederacy. Out on Belle Isle was Bellona Arsenal, and also in the town stood Richmond Arsenal, the Armory, countless government shops and plants. In the city, too, of course, were the executive and legislative offices. Virginia's stately, pillared capital now served the Confederate Congress, and not

far from the legislative halls stood the handsome Confederate
White House.

Richmond had changed a lot during the war. From a relatively quiet, lazy Southern city it had become a bustling, over-
crowded metropolis. Its denizens had slowly grown used to
throngs of outsiders, some of whom came from remote frontier
areas beyond the borders of the Old Dominion. They had
become accustomed to the hordes of government employees
who trooped daily to the makeshift offices near the capital,
who paraded on Franklin and Cary Streets, choked the lobby
of the Spotswood House, and talked in clusters on street cor-
ners, debated the editorials in the *Enquirer,* the *Sentinel,* the
Whig, the *Dispatch.* Richmonders were almost veterans of
the war themselves, so close had it come to them. And, consequently, they had a certain nonchalance about it; they wore it
well. Their city had lost its innocence, their country a good
deal of its agrarian isolation, and they were now at the heart
of a modern war effort. The factories, the bureaucracy, the
thousands of soldiers and office-seekers marked the change
from the old order to the new. From Richmond went the
orders to change a country, to transform it in the crucible of
conflict from an agrarian anachronism to part of the industrial-
izing nineteenth century. Richmond was the heart, and from
it arteries radiated to the whole South. It was an exciting place
to live in, an exciting place to work, and over its attitude of
blasé maturity always loomed the chilling prospect of desperate conflict.

An outsider ran the town and the country. Jefferson Davis
was a Mississippian, a planter-statesman in the best Southern
tradition. He had come to politics later than many, but his
earlier career had been sound. A West Pointer, a hero of the
Mexican War, he had served his state in the Federal House
and Senate and had gained fame as Franklin Pierce's Secretary

of War in the early 1850's. On the surface a cold, forbidding sort of man, Davis appeared to lack the necessary personal magnetism to make a good executive. But he was not without accomplishment. Although he did not lead Congress, did not win friends among the representatives and senators, he had organized a war, built a fighting machine out of virtually nothing, worked unceasingly to guard the constitutional freedom of a warring nation, and had patched together a government. Probably no one else could have done better, but Davis' legions of critics asserted that his administration bogged in military detail, in petty bickering, in endless redtape. Through it all Davis stood above the criticism, the carping, the comment to serve as the conscience of the South; he preached, pleaded and commanded his war. And of all Confederates he was the most dedicated to the cause. History would serve him ill for it was his lot to occupy a high place across battle lines from Abraham Lincoln, and the contrast would be devastating. But while he spoke without Lincoln's lasting appeal, lacked the Union President's rich and warm feeling for people, Davis possessed a brilliant legal mind, had a sound concept of his executive duties, and had invincible principles. And here was the tragedy: he was the perfect prototype of a Southern leader—honest, constitutional, gentlemanly, aloof. Against him in the judgment of history stood the century's giant, a man of sensitive spirit, saving wit, commanding eloquence. But Davis set much of Richmond's tone. His patriotism, determination, austere demeanor were Richmond's, too. His dogged prosecution of the war, his calm survey of the fields, his lasting devotion to General Lee were the hallmarks of a Richmonder. And as he was both Richmonder and Confederate, so were all the people in the town.

A frequent visitor was the city's favorite hero. General Lee, Virginian, had a special place in all Richmond hearts. He and his Army stood out in front of the capital and hurled back the Yankee minions; his army above all others in the Confederacy had gained smashing victories and gained for Southern arms the admiration of the world. And he was a paladin to suit the popular taste: stately, erect, with white hair and beard framing a genteel and refined face, with eyes that bespoke courtesy and kindness and compassion, his countenance and figure somehow also bespoke the daring of a Great Captain. He was now fifty-seven, but his exploits were those of a timeless Caesar. In manner, heritage, and achievement he was an unblemished product of the finest Cavalier tradition. He was one of the vanishing Southerners, those who fought for a South which lingered in fond legends and would go on to history in misty recollection of magnolias, and cotton—and General Lee. Some would later say that Lee was the last of the old-style generals, and his opponent in Virginia in 1864, Grant, the first of the moderns. Perhaps, but in daring maneuver, in desperate gamble, few fighting men, ancient or modern, could match him.

As he pondered the situation in the Richmond–Central Virginia theater in June, he planned a move which would deprive him of mobility but might stave off defeat. Hunter certainly would have to be stopped short of Lynchburg, and this necessity dictated that reinforcements would go to Breck-inridge. Lee always acted on the principle that the weaker side in war must take the greater risks, and was willing to surrender his own mobility in favor of a grand diversion which might relieve pressure on the Confederate capital. Now that Grant stood so close to Richmond and threatened a siege, and now that Sherman's legions daily sliced deeper into Georgia's heart, Lee realized that only the most heroic measures could save the Confederate cause. Attrition cut his own ranks every day and a limit apparently had been reached in manpower and material resources. The South marched steadily on a long downhill road which would lead inexorably to ruin unless some dramatic move retrieved it.

Lee's plans were daring and necessary. Strong reinforcements sent to Breckinridge might destroy Hunter's raiders, and then move north in a sweeping invasion of the enemy's country. The force detached from Lee's ranks might even threaten, perhaps occupy, Washington! If Washington were occupied it would not be for long, but any threat to the capital would produce panic in Northern hearts—it always had—and hence Grant might be forced to loosen his hold on the Richmond sector to save his own base. Occupation of Washington could have vital consequences abroad, too, where chances of recognition of the Confederacy seemed dead. And if nothing else could be done, a strong diversion northward would surely stave off the loss of Richmond and prolong the war. Lee felt he could hold his lines—heavily entrenched and protected by vast numbers of guns—with fewer men and decided he could spare a corps for use in his desperate gamble against the beginning of the end. On June 12 he called an old friend to Army Headquarters.

The friend was Jubal Anderson Early, newly created lieutenant general and newly assigned to command the Second Corps of Lee's Army.[20]

In what must have been one of the most exciting conferences Early ever had with Lee, he received orders to take his corps from the Richmond lines and move to the defense of Lynchburg, to break up Hunter's force and to do more if the possibility presented itself. Here was both boundless opportunity and terrible responsibility. Early could act on his own, command a separate army, and reap the credit for great deeds done. But failure would be on his head, too, and failure might involve consequences so dire as to appall men of feebler confidence—the loss of the Second Corps might mean the loss of Richmond.[21]

Lee made his selection of command and commander after much deliberation. The Second Corps certainly should go. Formerly the old Army of the Valley, many of its men were familiar with each rill of the Shenandoah, many were Valley men longing for a chance to see home and to make certain of the safety of their families. The corps, too, had no fear of hard marching; Stonewall had preached the virtues of maximum effort until none of the men realized anything else could be given. And since the campaign against Hunter would doubtless involve hard marching and short rations, Stonewall's boys were the obvious choices. But what about Early?

Forty-seven years old, a lifelong bachelor, not tall, sporting a grizzled beard and curling locks, the sharp-eyed Jubal had considerable reputation in the Army. There was much to commend him. A West Pointer (class of 1837), Jubal had been assigned to the artillery, fought against the Seminoles in Florida in 1837–1838, then against the Cherokees. He had resigned his commission as First Lieutenant in July, 1838, to take up the practice of law in Franklin County, Virginia. There he made a considerable impression at the bar, but suffered from an innate inadequacy as a businessman—he failed to collect from numerous clients. When the Mexican War began, he returned to the Army and participated in the campaign in the North Mexican States, was Acting Governor of Monterey, occasionally commanded an infantry regiment, but saw no real action. Early's non-combatants had been attached to the army under Zachary Taylor after the future president had won his plumes at Buena Vista. Still, Early came close to the greats in Mexico. He met and found fascinating Jefferson Davis, the Mississippi colonel who earned such a reputation at Buena Vista. "I was struck with his soldierly bearing," Early later recalled, "and he did me the honor of complimenting the order and regularity of my camp." With those few kind words, Davis gained the unending loyalty of one of the Confederacy's most devoted soldiers.

When the Mexican War ended, Early again went back to civilian life and his busy but financially unrewarding career as a Virginia barrister. The outbreak of the Civil War found him ready to take the field. He volunteered in the Virginia service, accepted a colonel's commission, and soon gained the admiration of superiors for his steady discipline, careful attention to details and growing aggressiveness. Soon promoted to the command of a brigade, Jubal led it with distinction at First Manassas, and it formed one of the main elements of General Joseph E. Johnston's Army when Johnston moved to oppose General George B. McClellan's advance up the Virginia Peninsula. Early received a severe wound at the Battle of Williamsburg, but returned to his brigade in time to participate in the Seven Days Battles around Richmond. At the battle of Malvern Hill he displayed a characteristic inability to understand terrain, lost a large portion of his brigade in the maze of trees, scrub growth and bad roads, but found them in time to form a line of battle after the action ceased on the field.

Attached to the division of General Richard Stoddert Ewell, which was in the corps commanded by Stonewall Jackson, Early's brigade took part in Jackson's campaign against General John Pope in central Virginia, went with Jackson on the famous flank march which culminated in the Battle of Second Manassas. In this campaign Early distinguished himself by firm leadership in several tight situations, saved his brigade during a terrifying night's exile across the Rappahannock from the remainder of the Confederate army, and fought with dogged determination in every action.

At the Battle of Sharpsburg on September 17, 1862, Early's

brigade guarded the left flank of the Army, and at the height of desperate combat Jubal summoned his men to hold against an entire Federal corps. Hold they did, and saved the flank of Jackson's corps and of the Army. The deeds of that day earned Jubal a promotion, and the wounding of Ewell and others during the campaigning from Second Manassas to Sharpsburg gave Early a division. As a division commander he did well. Constantly growing in command capacity, he grew equally as a fighter. Shortly, almost every Rebel in Lee's Army would concede that Early's division hit harder than almost any other, could be relied on in any emergency. That judgment went for Early, too, and General Jackson shared the opinion.

Although Jackson and Early were at opposite poles in viewpoint, they were temperamentally alike. Stonewall appreciated the blunt Jubal's love for combat, his readiness to commit his division—a rare quality, one hardly found in most generals. Jackson liked, too, Early's frankness, his complete lack of pretension, his honesty. Early's colorful, not to say ribald, language did not please the dour Deacon, but Jackson could forgive Jubal his cussing as long as he fought like Joshua. The two were never close—their views prevented that—but they had a vast respect for each other, and it lasted. Jackson's death after Chancellorsville was a personal blow to Early— he never forgot Jackson's lessons in war and tried always to emulate his mentor.

At a higher level, General Lee noted Early's developing competence with pleasure. By the beginning of 1863 attrition already had cut into the higher ranks of the Army of Northern Virginia, and the Commanding General always looked for talent. When he found a general who would fight, would administer his command with diligence, Lee cherished him. During the Gettysburg campaign, Lee noticed that Early's division did as well, if not better, than others, and that Jubal's men came out of the invasion with morale almost as high as when they went in. When, during the severe fighting in the Wilderness in May, 1864, Ewell and General A. P. Hill were out of action, Early had temporarily been in charge first of Ewell's Second Corps (Jackson's old command) and then of Hill's Third. Both times he did a workmanlike job—not brilliant, perhaps, but competent certainly. It was true that in the confusion of the Wilderness on May 6, Jubal had neglected to hit an exposed Union flank when General John Gordon called attention to it. But aside from this characteristic reaction to a subordinate's suggestion, Early's actions had been sound and prompt. And everyone had been under pressure in the Wilderness.

General Lee had to weigh carefully some curious quirks of character in selecting Early as commander of an independent expedition to the Shenandoah Valley. The previous winter Early had been out in the Valley in charge of an ill-starred campaign against a ranging Yankee cavalry force. While he handled the counter-measures as well as resources seemed to permit, there were indications that he misunderstood the use of cavalry and harbored lingering contempt for the mounted arm. This might well be a fatal trait in a general operating away from the main army and utterly dependent on cavalry for information. Perhaps, though, he had overcome this weakness. At least Lee could hope so.

Another weakness obviously had not been overcome. Early still acted a little too quickly on his own hunches, still gave too little attention to the views of subordinates, and still—in Lincoln's figure—took too much counsel of his ambition. Impetuous, quarrelsome on occasion, bitingly sarcastic, Early did not make friends among his subordinate commanders. So sharp and carping was his tongue, that lesser officers who suffered barbed thrusts in Jube's high, piping falsetto, could not see his military virtues. Possibly the caustic exterior cloaked a certain insecurity.

Some saw beyond the cantankerousness and glimpsed Early's wit, knew his occasional humor and his truly impressive cussing vocabulary. And those who bothered to know him, liked him. But he was hard to like, and it took work to keep on liking him. Relentless belief in his own ability, unstinting drive, and constant sniping at the achievements and often fancied derelictions of colleagues added to the difficulty. But he was a good fighter, and some brigade and fellow division commanders knew it. Brave, cool, steady under fire, Early could be counted a soldier's soldier, but not along usual Southern-gentleman lines. Past feats with the army had earned him the coveted promotion to lieutenant general and he thought it was certainly due him.

Early was no Jackson—none had risen in Old Jack's place —but of all the surviving higher officers, who had greater audacity, experience, and dogged tenacity? Doubtless these were the factors that brought Lee to the final decision. With the fate of the Confederacy possibly in his hands, Early would have to stick to his objective of making an effective diversion, all the while keeping his eye cocked on Richmond. This diversion, in keeping with the Confederate strategy of the offensive-defensive, envisioned a race down the Shenandoah Valley, swift passage to the Potomac and a sharp thrust at Washington. If all went well, panic in the Northern capital might produce detachment of Grant's strength or perhaps force him to a rash assault along Lee's entrenched lines. Either Yankee reaction would give Lee a chance for battle under circumstances of his own choosing.

Could Early do the job? He thought so, and when they learned of the orders, so did the veterans of the Second Corps. The Army of the Valley had been born again.

2

*

HUNTER HUNTED

VETERAN TROOPS are hard to fool. They can pretty well tell what the brass is planning almost before the brass knows—it becomes a matter of self-preservation and helps restore some of the balance between officers and men. The guessing game started in the camps of the Second Corps as soon as Old Jube called for the chiefs of the corps supply services. If he wanted a special conference with the Ordnance, Commissary, Quartermaster, Medical, and Engineer chiefs, something big was in the wind. No one knew that General Lee had given Early verbal orders earlier on June 12, alerting the corps for a swift march toward the Shenandoah, but every man lazing in the rest area near Cold Harbor, behind A. P. Hill's Third Corps, knew that Old Jube would move soon.

Lee always gave special care to the guidance of a new corps commander, and lest his verbal instructions be misinterpreted, he sent written confirmation the night of the twelfth.[1] The orders were specific and spelled out carefully the plans of the Commanding General. "Move," General Early read, "with the whole of the Second Corps toward the Shenandoah and prepare

to meet Hunter." Two battalions of the Corps artillery were
to go along.[2]

Early cherished no illusions about the strength of his force.
Whatever he did would have to be done by no more than 8,000
men, plus the artillery battalions—boasting twenty-four guns—
which were placed under the over-all command of Brigadier
General Armistead Long. But if his ranks were thin, if they
amounted only to the skeletons of the Second Corps he had
known, they were nonetheless some of the finest soldiers in
Lee's Army. With any luck at all, experience, the steadiness of
veterans, and speed ought to make up for the men missing.

Orders called for an early departure—happily reminiscent of
many handed down by Stonewall: march at 3 A.M., June 13.
In the lead would be the division commanded by reliable
Major General Robert Rodes, with John Gordon's and Dodson
Ramseur's following.[3] At the announced hour, Rode's men
moved out, and Early's columns filed swiftly from the Gaines'
Mill campsites.

The men marched well, as Early expected. The predawn air
was cool that Monday morning; there was a spring in the step
as the men anticipated some fierce blow at the enemy. Westward the column marched, passed through Mechanicsville,
crossed the Chickahominy at Meadow Bridge and kept on to
the Brooke Road, which took them northward from Richmond.
Settling down to route step, the men moved easily but steadily.
Old Jube meant business, no dawdling. On to the Plank Road
now, then northwestward to the Old Mountain Road. Where
were they going? Through the growing heat of that June day
the troops trudged on, clouds of dust choking the rear units.

The wagon trains kept well closed—and whatever Old Jube
planned must be important for the ordnance and quartermaster
wagons were numerous, indeed. As afternoon dragged on, the
corps came to familiar ground near the South Anna River.

After the columns covered some twenty-five miles Early finally gave the order to halt, and the troops made camp by the river near Auburn Mills.[4]

While the men were falling out of ranks, selecting likely places to sleep and building their campfires, Jubal and staff trotted to the Chewning house near the Mill and sought a night's lodging. Hospitably received, the general took time to ponder his route and to take stock of the first day.

Everything had gone as well as he could have anticipated. So many officers were new to the corps that Early had watched carefully for indications of trouble. Of the twelve brigade commanders who led at the opening of the Wilderness campaign, only one, Cullen Battle, now directed the same brigade. Attrition also had cut the ranks of field officers, and even at division level two faces were strange. John Brown Gordon and Stephen Dodson Ramseur had only recently taken charge of divisions. In one day Early could not discover much about the mettle of his new officers, but of Gordon and Ramseur he knew a good deal and expected more.

Through the gruelling test of the Wilderness campaign, Early had been in close contact with Gordon. And not all of their association had been pleasant. Early's penchant for rejecting the views of subordinates had led him to ignore an invaluable piece of intelligence from Gordon—intelligence which might have altered spectacularly the action in the Wilderness on May 6. This affair had resulted in bad blood between Early and Gordon, especially since Gordon's views finally gained the wholehearted approval of General Lee.[5] But Gordon's exploits had been so spectacular during the latter part of May 6, his command of Early's old division so competent, that Early had to overlook past grievances—especially since Gordon's experience exceeded that of the other division commanders, and the division contained elements of the old Stonewall Brigade as well as Early's own reliable brigade. The tall, statuesquely thin officer with flowing locks had much to commend him. His stern, soldierly look bespoke his real ability. If Major General and Lieutenant General could not cooperate, would not perhaps, the expedition could hardly escape disaster. Gordon and Early buried the hatchet—for a time.

What of Dodson Ramseur? Young—scarcely twenty-seven —he had displayed growing capacity for field command. As a brigade commander in the stern Wilderness testing, he had proved himself by steady and forceful leadership. When he attacked, he did so to make a mark. His men followed him and achieved under him. Youth might be a deterrent to divisional promotion in normal times, but the Army of Northern Virginia suffered the sear of attrition and times were anything but normal. Ability had become a scarce commodity; where it could be found, it must be rewarded. Lee had recommended Ramseur's rise with confidence and had thrilled the young man almost beyond expression with a personal commendation.[6] The wreath of a major general had come to him June 1, the day after his twenty-seventh birthday, and he had confessed his elation to his wife the day before the official appointment. He would do his whole duty, he wrote her, but would "be the more rejoiced on your account, first, because you will be pleased at the honors conferred on me, and, second, because I'll not be so much exposed."[7] If the boyish major general lacked experience, he at least had the virtue of valor, and inexperience might make him more malleable to Early's will—a real asset.

Brigade leaders were new, and Early would have to study them at more leisure, or the division commanders would have to tell him about them. Of the artillery chief Early knew much and had little doubt that Armistead Long would prove adequate to any test. From the time General Lee took command of the Army of Northern Virginia, until September, 1863, Long had been the general's military secretary. In that vital role he learned all that went on in high army circles, knew the mind of his chief as few others, and commanded the respect of Lee and of the President. Although Lee hated to part with him, he realized that Long's brilliant knowledge of artillery tactics made him an invaluable asset in the field and had reluctantly let him take charge of Second Corps artillery. Long had designated the batteries of Lieutenant Colonels William Nelson and Carter Braxton as those to go with Early, and Long's judgment was good enough for Jube.[8]

Cavalry had yet to join the corps, and Early postponed concern about the mounted arm.

Supplies stood to be well handled, since many of the men selected by Stonewall Jackson to produce food, shelter, transportation, ordnance, engineering, medical and other supplies still served the corps.

As the corps seemed to be running well, Early turned his attention to matters of intent. Where should he go from Auburn Mills? Information coming from the vicinity of Lynchburg was scanty. Just where Breckinridge was and what his situation Early did not know. Doubtless he did know that telegraphic communication with the western parts of Virginia had been interrupted; certainly he knew that Wade Hampton's and Fitz Lee's columns had spurred ahead of Breckinridge to intercept Sheridan's cavalry. Of their fate, he did not as yet have definite word. Breckinridge's condition was the pressing point. As a matter of fact, had Early known of Breckinridge's own confusion he could hardly have been inspired. Conditions at and near Charlottesville were unsettled, but it had begun to dawn on Breckinridge as early as June 8 that Hunter's objectives lay south of Charlottesville, and that possibly he aimed for Staunton.[10] A conglomerate of information poured into Lynchburg—the enemy was here, there, everywhere. His numbers were overwhelming; his numbers were thin; he intended this and that.[11] By the first day of action at Trevilian Station, Breckinridge probably knew that Hunter's men were too numerous for his command to handle. By then, however, he had high hopes for reinforcements, and he heard of Early's detachment to assist him almost as soon as Jubal received orders to go.

But Early could not open communication with Breckinridge; he did not know where the general was, nor where he intended to be. Without accurate information of Confederate or Union activities near Charlottesville, the supposed focus of operations, Early had to continue with his original plan of concentrating at or near that beautiful college town. Charlottesville had the virtue of guarding a junction of the Orange and Alexandria and Virginia Central Railroads, and thus had obvious strategic value. Early would have liked to use the Virginia Central in getting to Charlottesville, but Sheridan ranged somewhere along the line between Richmond and Gordonsville and service had been interrupted. As things stood that night of June 13, Early would have to wait until he was much closer to Charlottesville to find out what was going on and what he might have to do.

As light streaked the eastern skies, the gray columns were again in motion, the veterans marching steadily. Now the men had some notion of what the old man had in mind. Direction shifted with the South Anna, and the infantry moved along a line roughly parallel to and north of the stream; northwestward heading meant the corps moved toward the Shenandoah. With high hearts Stonewall's old command thought of home, the rolling hills of the valley, the Blue Ridge waiting in stately splendor. Somewhere beyond Charlottesville, according to marching gossip, lay the blue minions of the Virginia Yankee,

David Hunter. The old Army of the Valley should make short work of him and his men.

The day was warmer than the one before. Early had shifted his lead elements, and Ramseur's men set a pace which shrouded their following comrades in choking dust. Conditions were slightly improved by the fact that the commanding general directed his wagon trains to move by roads to the southwest, which helped a little to keep the dust down.[12] By late afternoon the corps had entered war-torn Louisa County, and camps were established for the night at Gardiner's Cross Roads. Still Early heard nothing of Breckinridge, or of Hunter's whereabouts. He gave some thought to aiding Hampton's cavalry against Sheridan, but probably learned that night of the Union defeat two days before—if so he doubtless marched toward Gordonsville with easier mind.[13]

Anxious to come to grips with the enemy, and concerned at operating in a thicker than usual fog of war, Early had the corps in the road at sunrise on the fifteenth, Gordon's men in the lead. Heat shimmered along the road, the men were grimed and sweaty, but in high spirits.[14] Early rode at the head of the infantry, urging on the van. About 8 A.M. he trotted into Louisa Court House, found a telegraph office and dispatched an impatient message to General Breckinridge, whom he apparently thought still near Charlottesville:

> Louisa Court-House, June 15,
> 1864—8 A.M. (Via Gordonsville.)
>
> General Breckinridge:
> Will be near Mechanicsville, Louisa County, to-night, and near Charlottesville to-morrow night. What is the state of things in the Valley? Let me hear from you via Gordonsville. Sheridan's force has been driven back from this place by Hampton. Nothing new from Richmond. . . .
>
> J. A. Early,
> *Lieutenant-General.*[15]

Without waiting for word from Breckinridge, Early pushed on. Five miles beyond Louisa Court House he passed near Hampton's battlefield at Trevilian Station, and as the warm day [16] wore on, he turned his columns southwestward and aimed at Charlottesville. Camps were made that night near Valentine's Mill. Early established headquarters at West Mills, where he fretted through the hours until dawn of the sixteenth.

Rodes' veterans took the lead as the men moved out at sunrise. The day was less hot than the previous ones, the country rolling and lovely as it approached the Blue Ridge foothills. As the men toiled upland they apparently left more of their cares behind; bantering raillery could be heard along the ranks.

Early's impatience prodded him on; he spurred his mount and galloped ahead of his troops. Through Mechanicsville he sped, thence to Charlottesville. In Charlottesville he found a telegram from Breckinridge in Lynchburg; Hunter, warned Breckinridge, was in Bedford County, twenty miles from Lynchburg and was approaching fast. If the great Confederate depot were to be saved, Early must come swiftly.[17]

Everything changed for Jubal. Now he knew where the enemy was, where Breckinridge was, what was going on. Now he could act with decision. While the corps closed on Charlottesville, Early established headquarters near the University of Virginia and made a quick survey of communication and transportation facilities. He found that fortunately the railroad and telegraph lines between Charlottesville and Lynchburg were now in working order. Good news, but Early's problem hinged on time: Hunter was twenty miles from Lynchburg, the Second Corps sixty. The decrepit Orange and Alexandria Railroad offered the obvious answer, but only if managed efficiently.

Previous experience with the superintendent of the O&A had fixed firmly in Jubal's mind the absolute unreliability of the line. This well-developed distrust made him overcautious. He wired Breckinridge at 11:40 A.M. on the sixteenth to "send off at once all engines and cars of the Orange and Alexandria Railroad to this place, including everything at its disposal. I will send troops as soon as I get cars. . . . See that there is no lack of energy in railroad management, and give me information from time to time." A frenzied hour's activity heightened Early's concern, and he admonished Breckinridge once more about trains: "Let me know what the railroad agents can and will do," he telegraphed his harried subordinate, "everything depends upon promptness, energy, and dispatch." Lest anyone misunderstand his grim determination, he spelled out carefully what would happen if the railroad officials failed. "Take the most summary measures and impress everything that is necessary in the way of men or means to insure the object. I have authority to direct your movements, and I will take the responsibility of what you may find it necessary to do. I will hold all railroad agents and employés responsible with their lives for hearty cooperation. . . ." [18]

By two-thirty in the afternoon Early had learned a bit more of Lynchburg's dire straits. Breckinridge confirmed the menacing advance of the enemy and urged Early's rapid arrival. He would come, he promised, but could not start until all the trains arrived from Lynchburg. Suspicion of the railroad officials made it seem imprudent to start trains in two directions at once; and even if he could trust the managers to avoid delays, his infantry had marched twenty miles that day and a total of eighty since leaving Richmond. Some elements of the corps were not yet closed, and those that were within easy distance must rest.[19] Nothing for it but to wait until morning of the seventeenth. Then, if all went well, the Second Corps would board the cars and thunder into Lynchburg in ample time to thwart Hunter's designs.

In one of his more high-sounding and mysterious phrases Early had announced that his "first object is to destroy Hunter, and the next it is not prudent to trust to telegraph." [20] Breckinridge could be pardoned if he harbored doubts of Early's capacity to destroy Hunter. Even if Jube arrived with his whole command with the first streaks of light on the seventeenth—a dubious possibility, indeed—there seemed every chance he would be too late. If Hunter advanced energetically, the Federals might be within artillery distance of Lynchburg by afternoon of the sixteenth and in the thinly held city by nightfall.

Energy, as Early had said, proved the crux of the situation. He who had it would succeed, and as things developed it came clear that Hunter had it not. On June 15 lead elements of Hunter's force crossed the Blue Ridge at the Peaks of Otter and took the road toward Lynchburg. By evening of that day he reported that his men were in Liberty, about twenty-four miles from their objective. They were on a direct artery to Lynchburg, and though the terrain was hilly and rough, the challenge of the Blue Ridge had been met and overcome. Nothing lay between the Union Army and the Confederate base save the worn and shattered forces of Generals John McCausland and John Imboden. Dogged as were these Rebels, they had been unable to do more than slow Hunter's columns and could hardly be expected to do that much longer. It was time to press directly forward. Hunter halted; some of his subordinates worried lest fancied Rebel forces strike their flanks and an urge to concentrate seized all the commanders. [21] While Hunter called in the outlying units, he put those at hand to the conscience-salving chore of tearing up the Virginia and Tennessee Railroad. A thorough job of wrecking consumed most of the sixteenth. Only a portion of his ranging cavalry—some of Averell's troopers—engaged McCausland that day, and by nightfall the whole Federal force had marched a scant seven miles beyond Liberty.[22]

Indecision settled over Hunter's headquarters during the night of the sixteenth–seventeenth. Although the country was high and hilly, the heat's oppressiveness seemed to creep into Hunter's thoughts. Rumors came to him in unhappy profusion. Some reports comforted with the word that Lynchburg was lightly held by convalescents, old men, and scratch units of militia, that its citizens were stampeding in panic; other reports placed all the Confederate troops in West Virginia in Lynchburg under formidable General Breckinridge and added to his fancied legions 20,000 reinforcements speeding from Richmond. In the alien, heavy darkness, Hunter wondered at the truth. While he knew he had to go on, caution born of the night's fantasies made him start his 200-wagon supply train toward safety beyond the mountains. This was the action of a psychologically beaten man. It remained now for time and Jubal Early to beat him in fact.

At 2 A.M. on the seventeenth Jubal started the finish of Hunter.

Weary troops had barely dropped to sleep in strung-out camps near Charlottesville when Jubal had them awakened— by 2 A.M., grumbling, and stumbling around in the dark, men of Ramseur's and Gordon's divisions were marched to the railroad. There the men saw evidence of the old man's hard labors —lines of cars, flaming, puffing engines. At last the footsore infantry would get a chance once again to taste war's modern conveniences. Amid much confusion, conflicting shouts and baffling orders, the columns formed to board. And then came the waiting—the interminable waiting that marked the biggest part of a soldier's life. Early chafed, his quartermasters fumed, and the railroad officials dallied. Things were not quite in order;

other trains were coming.[23] Streaks of light broke in the eastern
sky, and as the sun came into full view Early's patience wore
to the thinnest edge. Every minute counted—perhaps even now
the Second Corps was too late!

Finally, in full daylight, after Robert Rodes petulantly demanded first place in the advance, Ramseur's men were ordered
to climb aboard the cars—passengers, freight, box and stock—
and as soon as they were loaded some of Gordon's men followed.[24] The remainder of Gordon's division—only one
brigade was entrained—plus all of Rodes' command were to
march along the roadbed until trains could be sent back for
them. The artillery and wagons were directed to move as
swiftly as the condition of the horses would permit by direct
roads. Early ensconced himself in the lead train with some of
Ramseur's men and kept an anxious eye to the southwest.[25]

Although the trains rocked along at their best speed, the rails
were so worn, the bed so uneven and the cars so rickety that
progress seemed glacial. The sixty miles to Lynchburg ought
to have been covered in three hours at the most,[26] but the
morning dragged on as North Garden Depot, Rockfish Depot,
Arrington Depot faded slowly behind the last cars. Finally
Amherst Court House swung into view, then McIvor's Depot
and at long last, after a straight run of a few miles, Lynchburg.
When Early saw the hilly city's domes and spires the sun was
an hour past meridian. So late, so late! Who would meet the
trains? Confederates or Yankees? Anxious ears strained for
the sound of cannon. Nothing. Was this the caprice of acoustics
in the Lynchburg hills, or the ominous silence following capture? Or did it mean that decision had yet to come?

No resistance met the trains, and when Early's engine rattled
into the station, Confederates greeted the reinforcements. Early
had come in time!

The General ordered the trains back to pick up the remainder of his corps, and then sought out Breckinridge. He found him bedridden, suffering the effects of an old wound aggravated by a fall from a horse at Cold Harbor.[27] But the defense of Lynchburg had not gone unattended. Fortunately for Breckinridge, his old friend, General Daniel Harvey Hill, was in the city and had offered his services during Breckinridge's disability. Hill had undertaken to build the defenses, and offered to give Early a tour of the works he had constructed.

A potentially sticky situation, this, because Early had no great admiration for Hill, and Hill's position was unofficial. But Early proceeded to solve the dilemma as best he could. First he displayed his orders to Major General Breckinridge and received his junior's instant assurance of full cooperation; then he telegraphed Richmond for authority to assign Hill to the command of Breckinridge's troops.[28] Early happily noted that his old subordinate, General Harry Hays, was in town convalescing from a wound received at Spotsylvania and had offered his own able services in setting up a defense. Hays could be trusted to be thorough and calm. Hill at least could be trusted to be thorough.

As soon as the amenities were finished at Breckinridge's headquarters, Early and Hill began a tour of Lynchburg's defenses and a reconnaissance of the enemy's positions. Immediately Early had serious misgivings. Hill's lines were drawn right at the city limits. His works ran in a broken line around the southwestern, western, and northern edges, and his main strength had been concentrated on College Hill. Here, the eminence crowned with a few guns, Hill intended to make his stand against Hunter's strongest force, known to be approaching from the southwest on the Salem Turnpike. The Forest Road, leading in from the west, Hill would cover as best he could. The entire series of works stretched for more than a mile, and since Breckinridge's command had so few men for duty, Hill had been forced to put militia units, invalid troops, shattered remnants from the Piedmont fiasco, and the VMI cadets in various parts of the line. Considering Confederate strength, Hill had drawn the best line possible, but Early saw at once that its location would expose the city to enemy artillery fire and should the Federals advance determinedly, the closeness of the works would mean fighting literally in the streets. Now that more men were at hand, he determined to push the defensive lines out, and at the same time to scout the possibility of attacking.[29]

Early and Hill rode forward on the Salem Turnpike, toward Imboden's last known positions. The cavalry leader's battered men were still hanging on Hunter's flanks, nipping at his front and employing every possible delaying tactic to slow him down. The road from Lynchburg curled through hills, led across streams, skirted gorges. Finally the two generals heard the pop-popping of skirmish fire and the occasional booming of cannon. About four miles from Lynchburg, Early got his first look at the enemy. The Federals had shoved Imboden's ragtag force back to a position near a Quaker meetinghouse.

The stone meetinghouse stood on the crest of a ridge overlooking a stretch of the pike, and Imboden's men had taken cover close to the building behind some rail fencing. A few guns strengthened the position.[30] Stubborn resistance at the church had worked a minor miracle by the time Early got to the field: Imboden had forced Averell's cavalry to halt and call for infantry support. George Crook was coming up and deploying for a full assault.

Late in the afternoon—it must have been around 4:30 P.M. —Crook and Averell contrived a combined attack which threatened to flank the tiny Confederate force. Momentary panic seized Imboden's frazzled men and they started to break for the rear.[31]

As soon as Early had surveyed Imboden's hastily drawn line at the Quaker meetinghouse, he realized it could not hold for any length of time. A messenger spurred back toward Lynchburg to bring up the lead elements of Ramseur's division, bivouacking in front of Hill's works. Move, directed Early, to a redoubt he had seen, about two miles outside of Lynchburg; take position and hold the front.[32] Two Confederate guns were already unlimbered there and ready for action.

Everything hinged on speed. Imboden's men were finished; nothing could be done to rally them. A few scattered cavalry from other units tried to re-form, but the impressive Yankee lines of battle could not be halted without Ramseur. Back down the pike Early rode, urging his horse to a gallop. If he could only find Ramseur's men. . . . At last he saw them. Deploy! Advance as skirmishers! Swiftly the veterans of the Second Corps fanned out on both sides of the pike, the skirmish companies running ahead. Waving the men forward, Early rode with the skirmish line.

In the redoubt the cannoneers stood to the guns: load, ram, fire! Load, ram, fire! Still, Crook's Ohioans and West Virginians and Averell's dismounted troopers came at them. Surely the guns would be lost. Then, from behind the hard-fighting defenders, not far, came a muted bugle call, distorted by the heat, the firing, the fierce anxiety. What was it? The charge! Clearly the gunners heard it now; those who could spare a quick glance saw a sight to gladden their hearts for the rest of their lives: there in the swirling dust, the gunsmoke, the mass of onrushing grayclads, was the big white slouch hat of Old Jube leading the Stonewall Brigade to the rescue. The fire of battle lit his face; and as he reached the guns, he shook his fist at the enemy as he yelled, "No buttermilk rangers after you now, damn you. . . ." It was a decisive moment. With Jubal at hand and with Ramseur's two brigades on the field, the redoubt was held. A fierce counterattack shoved the Yankees back. On the pike the chastened bluecoats began a sullen artillery duel, and to the north on the Forest Road, McCausland slowly backed up ahead of a lethargic enemy force.[33] But fighting of consequence ceased for the day.

Early pondered the morrow. Encouraging as had been the day's deeds, he had serious worries. The rest of Gordon's division and all of Rodes' were slow in arriving—the Orange and Alexandria seemed to be justifying every suspicion. Wagons and artillery still dawdled somewhere between Lynchburg and Charlottesville. Counting Breckinridge's command, the scratch cavalry under Imboden and McCausland, everyone who could man the lines, Early scarcely mustered 7,000 men as darkness ended the fighting on the seventeenth.[34] His ranks were so thin he could barely hope to hold the line he worked desperately to establish during the night.

The new line covered the Salem Pike and bent slightly right, offering some chance to cover the Forest Road, although field works did not extend that far north. Early could not hope to splay his infantry across all the western approach to Lynchburg at any distance from the city, and had to gamble that the main enemy effort would come on the front where Crook and Averell were. If anything happened on the Confederate right, it would probably be a diversion, and McCausland with some of Breckinridge's infantry under Gabriel Wharton would have to hold it in check.

Lamps burned long at Headquarters, Army of the Valley, during the night of the seventeenth and eighteenth. Early's problems were myriad, and the tardiness of the rest of his divisions was but one of them. Richmond had rejected his plea for Hill's assignment to command, and countered with the disquieting information that in Hill's place Major General Arnold Elzey would arrive from the capital.[35] Long an invalid, Elzey had done his noble best to cope with commanding the relatively uncomplicated Department of Richmond. At Gaines' Mill he had suffered a hideous wound which had combined facial disfigurement with severe damage to his tongue. Almost unable to speak, he had nonetheless struggled diligently with his departmental tasks and had certainly laid honest claim to the major generalcy which had come to him in December, 1862. Richmond officials apparently felt that he had sufficiently overcome his disabilities to take the field. Early hoped so.

Elzey, at least, had experience and commonsense. He would arrive on the eighteenth, and take over Breckinridge's infantry until that officer returned to duty—which happily appeared imminent—and then some other command might be found for him. What about the cavalry? Here was an arm of the service which invariably baffled Early. What the exact duties of mounted men were he had never quite understood; his opinion of the dashing troopers he expressed concisely in the action at the redoubt on the afternoon of the seventeenth: "buttermilk rangers" they were, ranging always away from stern fighting to sip buttermilk in a quiet farmyard while charming lissome lasses with tales of martial valor. He was wrong about his cavalry and he would never admit it. McCausland's and Imboden's units were chewed up by long, hard fighting. Their men had been in the saddle or fighting on foot for weeks; their horses were worn and hungry and broken down. Discipline had suffered in the heat of constant combat; morale had eroded under constant retreat. All the troopers were bone weary and half asleep. They, like their mounts, had not found enough food, and their uniforms had been worn beyond recognition. If they looked demoralized, they were. But they had fought to get that way.

Even Jubal would have to admit that McCausland's and Imboden's men were short on buttermilk and long on combat.

They were the ones who had contested every inch of Hunter's advance,[36] had stalled him, made him careful. They had taken the punishment, had given Early the time he needed. If Jubal were grateful, he failed to show it. Instead, he awaited, with impatience matching Breckinridge's, the arrival of Major General Robert Ransom. Ransom had recently been assigned command of all the cavalry in Early's theater; and since Jubal harbored an abiding and unfair distrust of McCausland and especially of Imboden, anyone else would be welcome—anyone who could relieve the commanding general of all responsibility for the mounted arm. Had Early known more of Ransom, he might have been glad to stick with what he had.[37] But Ransom seemed a likely man to Jubal who liked the fact that the North Carolinian had commanded infantry under Longstreet—a sure indication that he would bring sound discipline to the whimsical horse soldiers.

In the meantime, Early had to deal with immediate crises of the night. Prudence dictated that the Confederate troops dig in, and orders went to all units to throw up dirt along the designated line. Easier ordered than done, for the red clay was stiff, slick, and hard to turn, but the Second Corps troops were by now old hands at digging and the lines took form.

Early had to curb his natural inclination to attack. Although fully committed to the theory that the inferior force must be the more audacious, he recognized that his force was too inferior. Should he attack in the morning, in an attempt to catch the Yankees unready, he might gain some initial success, but the outcome would probably go against him. Failure of the attack might lead to the wreck of his command and the consequent loss of the city he had come to protect. Much as he hated it, he decided he would have to wait for his artillery, for the rest of Gordon's men, and for Rodes' whole division. But weakness did not mean absolute impotence. If his lines could be made strong enough, he would invite attack.[38]

With vague hopes for the day, Early slept briefly. Up at 2 A.M., he rode to the front for a survey of progress on the fortifications and a look at the enemy.[39] The morning air was cool, but indications were that the day would again be oppressively warm. In the predawn hours reports came to Early that the Orange and Alexandria struggled still to bring in the rest of the Second Corps, and trains had been kept running all night. Good, but not good enough. The men had to come on. With daylight came an unexpected calm. At around 7 A.M. some Confederate guns on the Salem Pike opened a slow fire, probing Federal positions, but could stir up little reaction. Apparently Hunter had not make up his mind about an attack.[40] Early made use of the time to check the lines once again, saw to it that some of Breckinridge's infantry moved on a little to the right to be in supporting distance of McCausland on the Forest Road, noted that Harvey Hill's second line had been manned with the invalids, militia and other irregular units, observed that his fifteen or twenty guns were distributed as well as circumstances permitted along the front. Nothing to do now but await Hunter's pleasure.[41]

The wait would be long, for Hunter's resolution had steadily declined during the last twenty-four hours. Unsure of Lynchburg's condition, beset by conflicting intelligence, Hunter had developed a dangerously sensitive ear. During the night he had listened with unease to the rattle of railroad cars, the eerie wail of locomotive whistles, cheers, bugle calls and drum rolls. Each sound worked its own effect on the harassed Hunter, each meant more Rebels. Had someone told him that one engine and a few box cars made most of the noise by shuttling back and forth through Lynchburg, he probably would have not believed it. Heavy columns must be arriving to aid the enemy, and the real question remaining in Hunter's mind was: how many men had Lee sent against him? One way to find out was to conduct a forced reconnaissance of the Rebel lines; another, of course, was to await attack. Position and circumstance forced a move on Hunter. What kind of move baffled him. During the night he had not only lost contact with reality, but also with part of his command. On his left Brigadier General Alfred Duffié with his First Cavalry Division, had wandered off on the Forest Road—just where, or to what issue, Hunter did not know. Whatever plan he made for the eighteenth would have to include means of re-establishing contact with his left elements.

When he at last made up his mind to act, Hunter pulled himself together. His objective now was accurate information of Confederate strength and position; obtaining that, a decision about assaulting Lynchburg. Everything boiled down to reconnaissance tactics, and these Hunter understood. On his extreme right a road ran from Campbell Court House into Lynchburg from the south, in his immediate front the Salem Pike cut through enemy lines, and on his left—presumably in the uncertain grip of Duffié—the Forest Road ran into the town from the west. Other roads there were, but these three were within operating distance, and should be used to develop Rebel intent. The plan, then: scouting parties on all three roads, each party strong enough to exert serious pressure, perhaps to drain off reserves from the stronger parts of the enemy's line.[42]

Early in the morning of the eighteenth Hunter issued orders to put his plan into operation. But few things in war are as uncertain as reaction to battle orders.

Duffié, with the First Cavalry Division, anticipated orders to advance. Very early Saturday morning he shook out a

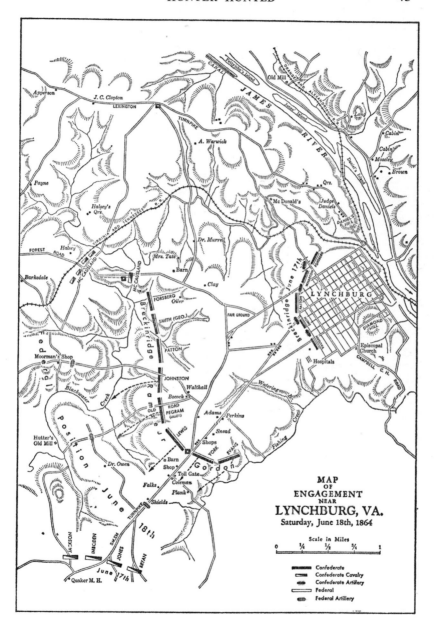

MAP
OF
ENGAGEMENT
NEAR
LYNCHBURG, VA.
Saturday, June 18th, 1864

Scale in Miles

0   ¼   ½   ¾   1

Confederate
Confederate Cavalry
Confederate Artillery
Federal
Federal Artillery

curtain of skirmishers, ran up some guns, and began shelling
McCausland's lines. Confederate skirmishers drew back slowly,
contesting each inch of ground as they had done for days.
The ground was poor for cavalry, and Duffié dismounted a
good portion of his men to fight on foot. McCausland's men
had refined delaying tactics to an art; occasionally a puff of
smoke would pinpoint a man lurking behind a tree, another,
another; here and there a crashing limb, a mushroom of earth
indicated the presence of horse artillery. But no line of battle
showed itself. Duffié pushed on, hoping that at least one of
the several messengers he had sent to Hunter would return with
definite instruction. In such alien land, faced by such stubborn
foes, he could hardly have been blamed for a certain caution.[43]
But steadily he kept shoving the Rebels back.

Finally, about four miles outside of Lynchburg, Duffié came
upon a railroad bridge, spanning the Virginia and Tennessee
tracks. His watch said it was 9 A.M., and still no word from
Army Headquarters. Obviously the bridge would be defended;
should he risk a heavy engagement? Without specific orders
changing his original assignment to probe the Forest Road,
Duffié made the soldierly decision to press forward. His expec-
tations were correct; Rebels contested the approach to the
bridge with unusual persistence. McCausland apparently had
called infantry to his support. But Duffié urged his men on,
and finally cracked the enemy front and sent the grayclads
scampering rearward. Before abandoning the field, the Rebels
partially destroyed the bridge, which forced Duffié to halt and
make emergency repairs.[44]

At 10:30 A.M. a messenger reached him from Averell with
orders: Do what had been done, but do it more vigorously,
urged the cavalry commander. Instantly deploying in force in
three columns—one each side of the Forest Road, one on the
road—Duffié did his best to obey instructions. Confederate

skirmishers dropped back, and the advance rolled on until suddenly Duffié spotted a line of Rebel works. They looked down on a crossing of Blackwater Creek and on each side of the road loomed large bastions, heavily manned and glinting with cannon.

Averell had promised reinforcements, but they had yet to come. The river banks were steep and the approaches treacherous. Duffié did the natural thing: he deployed his whole command in line of battle and made a careful reconnaissance of the Rebel lines. What he saw alarmed him.

> There was but one road by which a force could cross the stream, [he noted] and this road was commanded by two of their strongest fortifications. The enemy were strongly posted on the opposite bank of the Blackwater, while they opened a heavy artillery fire upon my cavalry from their fortifications.[45]

Ordering up a section of guns, Duffié shelled the bastions and temporarily silenced Confederate batteries. Encouraged, he ordered an attack by the Fifth New York (Lincoln) Cavalry and two squadrons of the Twentieth Pennsylvania. After partial success, the charge broke and the men fell back, badly chopped up. The Fifteenth New York Cavalry tried a demonstration on the right, but met a similar fate. It was well past noon now, heat eddied up from the creek bottoms, troopers lay under what little cover was available and cursed their heavy blue uniforms, the climate, the officers and the Rebels at the bridge. They could not go forward, and Duffié knew it.

On a field note pad he scrawled a dispatch to Hunter's adjutant:

Hdqrs. First Cav. Div., Dept. of West Virginia,
In the Field, near Lynchburg, Va., June 18, 1864.

Lieut. Col. Charles G. Halpine,
Assistant Adjutant-General, Dept. of West Virginia:

Sir: I have carried out your orders, in engaging the enemy on the extreme left. I attacked him at 12.30 P.M., and drove him into his fortifications. Have been fighting ever since. Two charges have been made, and the enemy's strength fully developed in our front. His force is much superior to mine. All my force is engaged. The enemy is now attempting to turn my right. I shall send a force to check him. I do not communicate with Averell on my right.

Respectfully, &c.,

A. N. Duffié,
Brigadier-General, Commanding.[46]

The attack on the right and another Rebel attempt to turn the left flank were stopped, but by the time Duffié had his line stabilized and in hand, the situation had radically changed. All afternoon the enemy had kept up contact; no further help came from Averell or Hunter. At 5 P.M. the Rebels opened a terrific fire of artillery and muskets, drove in Duffié's skirmishers and brought him swiftly to the front. From a hill he swept Lynchburg with his glasses. The town lay a scant two miles away, and he could see long columns of grayclads marching out along the Forest Road; the hoot of trains and snatches of martial music convinced him that the Rebels were heavily reinforced. Nervously Duffié dug in and awaited orders. What had happened to the rest of the army he did not know, though firing had been heavy from time to time during the afternoon. Shortly after 7 P.M. he happily received word from Hunter that the army was retreating and he should pull back.[47]

Duffié had been badly fooled, as had Hunter. McCausland and Gabe Wharton's tiny infantry brigade had marched, countermarched and fought without substantial help most of the day. Their brilliant bluff saved Early's right. On his center and left, he did his own bluffing.

For a portion of Saturday morning, Early could hardly believe what happened—or what failed to happen. Hunter surely would lash the Rebel lines, anyone would. But nothing save lazy Confederate cannonading occupied the early hours.

Word finally reached Field Headquarters [48] of an enemy
reconnaissance on the Campbell Court House road but this
was easily handled by some cavalry. Apparently the scouting
party had little stomach for its work.[49]

Near Early's main position at the redoubt nothing of consequence happened until about 11 A.M. By then Jubal's patience
had run out. He determined to test the enemy front, possibly
with the hope of finding a center weakened by detachments to
both flanks. In positions near the Salem Pike, Confederate
guns suddenly belched flame, jumped from battery, and were
wreathed in smoke. The barrage raged furiously for a time, and
then from the Rebel works streamed Ramseur's and Gordon's
men. Down a ridge near the pike they charged, and through
the roar of cannon came the thin, shrill Rebel Yell. Nobody
could have been more surprised than Hunter and the units in
his front line near the road. Brigadier General Jeremiah
Sullivan's First Infantry Division broke under the initial shock,
and some of his units fled toward the rear. Only the fortuitous
return to the field of some troops sent to the Campbell Court
House road saved the situation. With reinforcements, the
Yankee line stiffened, straightened, and counterattacked.
Early's men finally were shoved back to their works, but not
beyond them. Skirmishers again moved to forward rifle pits,
artillery boomed occasionally, and the sitting war continued
through the heat of the afternoon. Neither side resumed the
offensive.

But Early's sortie to prod Hunter into a general assault had
results which Jubal could hardly have expected: it convinced
Hunter that his army had beaten off a major offensive. And
that further unnerved the Federal general.

Jubal still planned a fight. Late in the day the overworked
railroads brought in the remainder of the Second Corps. Rodes'
men streamed through Lynchburg's hilly streets and were

directed to take the Forest Road and reinforce McCausland. Rodes' division it was that Duffié saw marching toward Blackwater Creek. And the arrival of Rodes, amid the hooting, shouting and gaiety which so chilled Duffié, put the finishing touches on Hunter. So many men coming meant only one thing: outnumbered, the Federals must retreat. For Hunter, the Battle of Lynchburg was ended.

For Early, it still raged. With all of the Second Corps now at hand, the time had come for a Confederate attack—even though Early's guns yet toiled toward Lynchburg. Hunter's army outnumbered the Rebels, but the opportunity to strike a hard blow ought not be missed. Obviously the Yankee commander had lost most of his determination, and his command appeared scattered and confused. In these circumstances a sharp attack might break up his army and distribute it far and wide over central Virginia. Early pondered the obvious question: when should he attack?

His combat instinct told him to burn no more daylight, to assail the enemy at once. Aggressive, dauntless John Gordon echoed the theme: attack now. Tactically the time was ripe, for the enemy's own offensive spirit had been spent and the Federals lay behind field works, content to watch and wait. Everyone in Lynchburg expected that their deliverer would smite the vandal Hunter in righteous punishment. Early's troops expected to be ordered forward.

But Early took time for circumspection. General Lee had not charged him with responsibility to be reckless, even though he had urged a swift blow at Hunter.[50] More than ever before, Jubal knew the loneliness of command. Generals Ransom, Elzey, who had arrived during the afternoon, Breckinridge, Gordon, Ramseur, Rodes, all expected to attack. But theirs was not the responsibility. The decision was Early's, and he elected to wait for morning.

He was not afraid of Hunter, far from it. But several considerations dictated hesitation: first, any attack on Hunter must be delivered with maximum chance of success, else the expedition might suffer disaster and hence so might Lee; second, Early's men were tired by long marching and hard fighting—they needed a rest; third, the Second Corps' artillery was not up, but might be by daylight. If, as Gordon prophesied, Hunter was gone by then, Early would have to risk it. Meanwhile, the men must be put to work digging. The most overworked units would be replaced in the lines and given a chance to relax for a few hours.

So it happened that after dark the VMI cadets, newly come to Lynchburg, got a crack at front-line duty. For a brief time they had been assigned reserve positions in D. H. Hill's original lines, and had found themselves guarding a graveyard, bivouacked with the dead. But at about 10 P.M. came orders to move up; they would relieve some of Dodson Ramseur's spent veterans. As the cadets fell in, the commandant passed the word—quiet! To prevent straggling and the loss of direction, officers told each man to place his left hand on the cartridge box of the man in front, and in single file they moved up.

Finally, after marching what seemed endless miles over baffling ravines and ridges, the boys saw a redoubt standing blackly in the night. They marched in, the ragged defenders marched out "like the shadows of darkness," and not a word passed.

> The place was horrible, [noted Cadet John Wise] the fort was new, and constructed of stiff red clay. . . . There was no place to lie down. All that a man could do was to sit plump down in the mud, upon the low banquette, with his gun across his lap. I could not resist peeping over the parapet, and there, but a short distance from us, in a little valley, were the smoul-

dering campfires of the enemy. Wrapping my blanket about
me, its ends tucked under me, so as to keep out the moisture
from the red clay as much as possible, I fell asleep, hugging
my rifle, never doubting that there would be work for both of
us at daybreak.[51]

Behind the Federal lines, too, there was activity. Hunter
decided during the afternoon that he would fall back under
cover of darkness, and sent orders to his various commands.
Some of his subordinates were dismayed, but hardly surprised.[52] By a little after 9 P.M. Hunter's columns were on the
roads toward Salem, a line of skirmishers still keeping up the
campfires and holding the front. Noise of the retreat could be
heard in the Confederate trenches, and Early faced squarely
the problem of whether to launch a night attack. He wanted
to, but by the time the enemy's move was reported it was
past midnight and, according to Early's own account, "it was
not known whether he was retreating, or moving so as to
attack Lynchburg on the south where it was vulnerable, or to
attempt to join Grant on the south side of James River. Pursuit
could not, therefore, be made at once, as a mistake, if either
of the last two objects had been contemplated, would have
been fatal." [53] When all possibility of error had been eliminated
by scouts, it was daylight and Hunter had stolen a night's
march.

Relieved of any chance of error, Early ordered a pursuit as
quickly as his troops could get out of the ditches and into the
roads. Straight after the retiring enemy went the Second
Corps, Ramseur and Gordon following them as closely as
possible on the Salem Turnpike. Arnold Elzey, in charge of
Breckinridge's little band now part of the Army of the Valley,
moved on the Forest Road, and on the far Confederate right
Ransom—in charge of McCausland's cavalry—must range
ahead toward Liberty or the Peaks of Otter in an attempt to

seal off the Yankee retreat. Breckinridge, almost ambulatory, was asked to ride with Early and lend his wise counsel as the day progressed.

Dust hung over the pike as Ramseur's and Gordon's men swung along; the heat grew stifling, but the sweating infantry covered ground well that Sunday morning. If Hunter lagged at all, he would be caught.[54]

Early and his staff rode alongside the column and the general noted that the regiments were well closed. By nine-thirty in the morning Early was in New London, some ten miles from Lynchburg. Evidence of hasty enemy withdrawal could be seen everywhere, and Early took occasion to telegraph General Lee what had been accomplished and what was planned:

New London, June 19, 1864—9.30 A.M.

General:

Last evening the enemy assaulted my lines in front of Lynchburg and was repulsed by the part of my command which was up. On the arrival of the rest of the command I made arrangements to attack this morning at light, but it was discovered that the enemy were retreating, and I am now pursuing. The enemy is retreating in confusion, and if the cavalry does its duty we will destroy him.

J. A. Early,
Lieutenant-General.

General R. E. Lee. (Care of General Bragg).[55]

The thrust at the cavalry was scarcely deserved, considering all that McCausland and Imboden had been doing, but reflected clearly Early's firm suspicion of his troopers—a suspicion he would retain to the detriment of some future operations.

In the afternoon, after his men were whipped by marching

in the withering heat, Hunter called a halt near Liberty. At about 4 P.M. Early's advance overtook some of Averell's tiring troopers and drove them rapidly through the little town.[56] The skirmish was sharp and killed a good number on both sides. But Early's full strength had not come up and the attack sputtered out in the gathering dusk.[57]

Early knew that Hunter would spare no effort to escape through the Blue Ridge, and that if he succeeded, there would be little chance to wreck his command. The infantry, of course, could do no more than press the Yankee rear guard; Hunter must be caught by Ransom's troopers.

Everything seemed to go wrong for the cavalry. Imboden had been ordered to move on the Campbell Court House road toward Liberty, while Ransom and McCausland followed Duffié on the Forest Road. Imboden missed his orders and Ransom missed his road. Consequently, the bedraggled troopers drifted into Liberty after Ramseur's men had pushed the Federals through the town. If the troopers could do anything with efficiency, Early had yet to see it!

After venting some pent-up spleen on the hapless horse soldiers, Early considered reports coming to him of Federal operations. Instead of sticking strictly to his route of advance, Hunter had varied his retreat roads and moved due west on the Virginia and Tennessee tracks. He did not diverge northward toward the Peaks of Otter, but plodded straight toward Buford's Gap and Salem.[58] Shrewd, indeed, for now he would have several avenues of retreat to choose from once through the curtain of the Blue Ridge.

No time to lament the ill fortunes of the nineteenth; Early gave orders rapidly. The aim of all strategy is to limit enemy opportunities to those desired by the strategist: Early wanted Hunter pinned to one road, encircled and cut to bits. First Hunter must be deprived of the vantage of maneuvering ground, then intercepted. To prevent his moving north toward Fincastle or Buchanan, Early sent Ransom back to the road to the Peaks of Otter with orders to cut through the Blue Ridge there and sit on Hunter's routes northward from Buford's. Gordon's men were put in the van as the infantry drew the assignment of pressing Hunter's rear guard. Marching and fighting promised to be a little less wearing for the heat abated somewhat, but the dust still billowed and parched.

Closely the Southern infantry followed Hunter's retiring cavalry screen, nipping at it several times during the morning. In the afternoon of June 20, heavy skirmishing broke out near Buford's Gap—the Federals deployed to hold the Gap, and Early tried to flank the defenders by sending Gordon to the left and Rodes to the right. The ground was confusing, the mountainside precipitous, and most of the day was gone before any formation could be achieved. Early reluctantly called off the fighting after dark.[59]

Everything depended on speed. Rodes was to move out long before dawn and endeavor to get behind the enemy, or at least intrude upon his retiring columns. But speed seemed the one thing Early could not generate. His messenger, bearing orders to Rodes to take the lead on Tuesday morning, became confused and Rodes failed to move as planned. Not until long past sunrise did his columns march; by then Federal dust could be clearly seen fading westward.[60]

The commanding general must have been increasingly concerned that his troops could not keep up the pursuit. He had moved from Lynchburg without his trains; many of the men were hungry, and Rodes' whole command had not had an issue of rations for three days.[61] Fatigue, coupled with hunger and thirst, played a major role in slacking the pace of the Second Corps.

Some of the men were luckier than others in matters of food.

Rodes' men suffered, perhaps, but on the twenty-first Gordon's troops were padding along the dusty road as thirsty and hunger-ridden as mortal men could be, when before them loomed a vision to beggar the imagination.

> We noticed several ladies standing on the side of the road [recalled John Worsham of old Company F, 21st Virginia Infantry.] And when we came nearer we saw two beautiful young ladies and their maids and near them were two huge wash tubs. The young ladies gave us an invitation to come forward and partake of some ice water and brandy julep. The men needed no second invitation; the head of the column moved up, the young ladies handed each man a drink, which was received eagerly, with many grateful wishes for their future welfare. I was told that the tubs were repeatedly emptied and filled. This was the biggest julep treat of my experience.[62]

Early received some good news about midday: McCausland's men had at last ridden into a Federal train, cut it up fairly well and captured a good number of enemy guns. McCausland could not hang on to them all since the enemy brought up reinforcements, but he spiked those left behind. The best news to come to Early that day, though, was that Hunter had turned off from his route toward southwest Virginia and headed for Lewisburg in the far western part of the state. To the perceptive Jubal this meant that Hunter could not stop until he reached the Kanawha—terrain, provisions, and roads would force him to the river.[63]

Hunter had not missed the portent of his route. He debated various roads, almost decided to retire northward through the valley of the south branch of the Potomac, but changed his mind when, as Hunter himself reported, "it was objected that by this road the troops would find it impossible to collect necessary supplies and run risks of being cut off by the enemy coming in by way of Staunton and Harrisonburg. In favor of

the route via Lewisburg to Charleston, Kanawha, it was urged
that the road was clear and practicable, and that while the
country would furnish little or nothing in the way of supplies,
yet we had ample stores at Meadow Bluff and Gauley River.
As the question of supplies was one that involved the existence
of the army the Kanawha route was decided upon. . . ." [64]

If not all had been done to Hunter that Early could have
wished, his expedition had been intercepted, beaten and driven
out of the theater of Northern Virginia. Early could take comfort in the knowledge that his sixty-mile pursuit from Lynchburg had accomplished the first phase of his assignment—driving Hunter out of the Shenandoah Valley, out of the campaign,
and for several weeks out of the war. Now he must ponder
phase two of his instructions from Lee.

3

---*---

INTO THE VALLEY

SOLDIERING SOMETIMES had its compensations. It was hard life most of the time, marching, fighting, starving, but now and then there were days to remember fondly, days to dim the horrors, the weariness, the drudgery. For Dodson Ramseur's men, Wednesday, June 22, 1864, would be cherished as such a day. The night before, most of the division had drifted into camps around Botetourt Springs, and when daylight came the men glimpsed their Elysian surroundings. They were in one of Virginia's resort spots, a spa which before the war catered to the whims and caprices of the gentry and their ladies who gathered to "take the waters" and to mingle with the socially prominent. The springs worked wonders on the constitution, the society revived the spirit, and the scenery restored the soul. Blue-green mountains, rugged, serenely lovely, cradled the springs in the happy isolation of a verdant valley. In all of Virginia there were many splendid resorts, many stirring vistas, but to the road-worn Second Corps none could compare with Botetourt. The little hamlet and the water stood out that morning in warm, mountain-clear sunlight. Without marching orders, the grimed veterans dashed to the springs, ran pell-mell into the water, and the whole valley rang with shouts and laughter.

Some soldiers speculated that Old Jube had called an unnatural halt here for personal reasons. Hollins Institute stood near at hand and rumor had it that one of bachelor Early's old flames taught in the female college. Obviously he stalled the campaign while he warmed over old amatory coals! [1]

While his men disported themselves in the ways of the gentry and pondered his romantic nature, Early reviewed the military situation with his generals. Hunter was now running and was being prodded into the western Virginia mountains by Ransom and McCausland. He had taken a road which guaranteed his absence from action for weeks. Since Hunter was disposed of, Early must now make a difficult decision: Lee had intrusted him with secret orders and a mission of such importance that the Richmond papers and the Confederate telegraph service had been forbidden to mention it.[2] If Early thought it could be done, he could take the Army of the Valley northward, cross the Potomac and threaten Washington.

What his subordinates thought, Early did not record. His own mind was made up by the time the army reached Botetourt. Small as was his force (even with Breckinridge's men, he counted no more than 12,000 muskets) war-weary as were the men,[3] and short as were their rations, the army would move north. The possibilities of glittering achievement, glory in good measure, the chance possibly to sack the Yankee capital, were not the deciding considerations. Doubtless they crossed Early's mind, for a man of ambition could not ignore such attractions, but he based his final decision on stern military necessity.

General Lee had gambled at desperate odds, and Early knew it. Marse Robert thinned the ranks at Petersburg almost beyond holding, in the hope of real achievement by Early's army. True, Lee put the final decision squarely up to Jubal—he could return to Petersburg if he thought it best. But Early knew enough of Lee's audacious nature to realize that he hoped the Army of the Valley would go north and do everything possible to take pressure away from Richmond. That alone would justify the risk of detachment; return to the lines would gain nothing and confess a reckless risk.

Understood in Lee's terms, then, the situation left Early no real choice. This point was made clear to the generals assembled in the relaxed surroundings at Botetourt. Orders were given—the army would move to Staunton, again a Confederate base, would reorganize, rest briefly, then strike northward over ground Jackson had made famous. The move would begin at dawn of the twenty-third. The generals took a long look at the spa, the mountains, the happy men—this might be the last resort some of them would ever see.

With Thursday's dawn Dodson Ramseur's men swung onto the macademized Valley pike, heading towards Lexington.[4] Marching steadily, the men approached Buchanan and by nightfall most of Ramseur's command had crossed the James. The other divisions closed on the river, and the men spent the waning afternoon gathering cherries from hapless farms nearby.[5]

Despite the extreme heat Early rode northwestward for part of the morning, tracking the Federal retreat. He wanted to be certain that Hunter plotted no sudden dash in behind the Confederates as they moved down the Valley. But cavalry reports had been accurate—the bluecoats streamed through the mountains, trains, guns, caissons, everything moving on ahead. They would not be back, but Ransom would nonetheless keep an eye on them for awhile. By evening, the commanding general had rejoined the army at Buchanan. Orders for the next day again put Ramseur's pace-setters in front and directed them toward Lexington.[6]

As the men marched northward Friday morning, Early was approached by one of Ramseur's staff officers. When he rode up and touched his hat, Early recognized Major Kyd Douglas, the handsome young Marylander who had been on Stonewall's staff. Jubal had a special fondness for the gay Douglas, had requested him for his own staff when he had commanded a division, and reluctantly left him with Ramseur, who needed competent aides. Douglas asked if there were time for an interlude in war. Would the General allow him to take some of the men from the Deep South a little out of the way for a look at a real Virginia wonder? On the route to Lexington that day the army would pass very close to the Natural Bridge, and this would be a splendid opportunity for a visit. Douglas could always be counted on for diverting ideas, and this one sounded so good that Early decided to go along with the men.

Years later Douglas recalled the excursion:

> I took several bands and have never forgotten the solemn effect of their music as it rose and swelled in volume, and filled the great arch and seemed to press against the sides of that cathedral dome, and then rolled along the high rocks that walled the ravine and died away in the widening wood.[7]

In the waning afternoon of Friday, the twenty-fourth, the lead elements of Early's army came close to Lexington, and as they topped the rise from which they had taken their last glance at VMI, the cadets slowed for a long look. The fist of war had smashed mightily against the town, and though still lovely in its idyllic setting, Lexington seemed stark and hurt. To the east the Blue Ridge still looked the same, their dark azure peaks grand and stately; the Valley pike still led northward to lush fields and friendly farms, and hills rolled gently westward still to sterner lands beyond the dim Alleghenies. But the town was maimed, its wounds gaped for all to see. Even from a distance, VMI's broken battlements loomed crazily, and

the parade ground no longer showed trim and clean. Dark
streaks on the light-colored walls were the ravages of fire. Not
far from the shambles of the Institute could be seen the black-
ened mass of timbers which once had been the handsome home
of Governor John Letcher. Despite the obvious efforts to erase
the marks of pillage, an atmosphere of gloom hung heavy over
Lexington.

Depressed and quieted, the army camped nearby for the
night.

Saturday morning Robert Rodes' men took the point of the
column, marched resolutely into Lexington and then diverged
a little from the main road through the gates of a small cemetery. The baleful notes of a dirge floated over the long lines of
infantry, and each man uncovered, reversed his rifle in marching tribute, and filed past the grave of Stonewall Jackson. So
little there was to see, a small mound of Virginia sod marked
by a tiny Confederate flag. But so much of his spirit still per-
vaded the army. . . . All the men admired Marse Robert, he
was the Grand Old Man, a great and commanding figure, a
peerless strategist. But Stonewall had been the heart of the
Army of the Valley, had given the men a mettle to set them
above friends and foes, an *élan* to mark them in the eyes of the
world. They respected Lee; they loved the strange professor
from VMI who took their last salute that morning. In the
silence broken only by the padding bare feet of the men, some
forgotten lines of Tennyson flashed back into Kyd Douglas's
memory:

> They are here my own, my own;
> Were it ever so airy a tread,
> My heart would hear them and beat,
> Were it earth in an earthy bed:
> My dust would hear them and beat
> Had I lain for a century dead! [8]

No time for lingering memories, Jubal left the cadets to mourn the Institute and pushed the rest of the men rapidly toward Staunton. The next day, June 26, the army reached this important depot town and found the commanding general already there with headquarters hard at work. But the men received happy orders to pick campsites and take a rest.

While the troops relaxed and snatched what pleasure could be had, Early wrestled with serious logistical problems—problems confounded by poor communications and creaking rail lines. He noted with alarm that almost half the Army was barefoot, and there were limits even to tough-soled, corn-fed endurance. He had ordered a shipment of footgear sent to Staunton during the halt near Salem, but it had not arrived by the time the infantry streamed into town. Reminders were sent to the Quartermaster General in Richmond, and assurance came of imminent delivery.[9]

Some commissary stores ordered from Richmond depots and other points east had come to Staunton via Waynesboro, but Early could not yet rest easy about rations and forage. He would have to survey local possibilities.[10]

Shortly, though, the chief quartermaster, energetic John Harman, and his chief commissary, Wells J. Hawks, could report bountiful resources—the Valley burgeoned with its largest harvest for many years and fortunately the Federals had not made serious inroads into the fabulous Shenandoah granary.[11] This came as welcome news, for it meant that the Army of the Valley could not only feed itself, but might add to the pitifully thin food and forage reserve of Lee's Army.[12]

With supply problems at least temporarily solved, Early turned his attention to army organization. After a march of over 200 miles in fourteen days,[13] the men were broken down —"played out" said one grayjacket[14]—and various units suffered from illness and straggling. The horses for artillery and

wagon trains were suffering severely the effects of hard marching and short forage. There would have to be a general shaking
up of all units, and Early set about it with soldierly resolution.
The reorganization he conducted revealed a good deal about
Jubal as an independent commander; showed many of his real
strengths and certain questionable weaknesses.

He began with the infantry—a logical starting point for an
old line officer. On the march from the vicinity of Botetourt,
it became apparent that old Arnold Elzey, combative and loyal
as ever, simply could not endure the rigors of a hard campaign.
Early hesitated to tell Elzey what all could see, and for days
Arnold had toiled onward, face contorted, struggling for wind.
Finally, when part of the army reached Midway, he gave up.
To Jubal he confessed that he could not go on. Would Early
relieve him? Sad for Elzey but doubtless relieved that such an
awkward situation had been resolved, Jubal issued the orders.
With the army resting at Staunton, Early could now devote
some thought to replacing Elzey in command of Breckinridge's
infantry. Breckinridge, himself, had to be considered. He had
accompanied the army from Lynchburg, had contributed
generously of his experience, of his wide knowledge of the
people and ground, of his wisdom in strategic councils. Early
had come into Breckinridge's geographical department, and
the junior officer had yielded authority without hesitation; cooperation had been smooth and effortless. These considerations
were important to Early and he desired to give the former
Vice-President of the United States some duty commensurate
with his rank and station. If Breckinridge took charge of his
old troops, he would be just another division commander, with
few more than 2,000 men [15] under him. This hardly seemed
adequate. But another possibility occurred to Early—one which
had all the earmarks of a flash of genius. If he created a corps
for Breckinridge to command, a post of dignity and substance

would be the Kentuckian's, and if his own men and the division of General Gordon were put in the corps, two troubled units would be in trustworthy hands.

The trouble sounded petty, but to the rank and file there were valid reasons for discontent. Harry Hays' Louisianians had been consolidated with Leroy Stafford's into a brigade in Gordon's division, and all were now under Brigadier General Zebulon York—an old Yankee who had adopted Louisiana as his own.[16] Consolidation, even of men from the same state, rankled; nowhere was this better illustrated than in Brigadier General William Terry's brigade, also of Gordon's division. Terry led shattered but proud remnants of Allegheny Johnson's old command, among them the stalwarts of the Stonewall Brigade. Thin ranks made separate organization uneconomical, but economics mattered little to men who thought that their brigade alone among all units deserved a special place in the Rebel pantheon. Bill Terry, tactful and able, faced a serious problem in morale. Gordon, of course, faced a larger one in having to extract the best of two fractious brigades. Even the stubborn Georgian, practiced though he was in command, might find difficult the management of his division. Breckinridge surely could help, but he would have to devote some attention to his own little division, which also suffered its small dissensions. His troops, as loyal and hard fighters as a general could desire, were mountain men with a special individualism. They would contend fiercely for their mountain homes, die without whimper or regret, but if far removed from the Virginia hills they lost interest in campaigning, became "high privates" and went to visit their families. They were never deserters, just wanderers; they would return when fancy dictated. As long as Early's army operated in the bounds of the Shenandoah, and Wharton's and John Vaughn's boys could see the far vistas of the Alleghenies and the Blue Ridge, their morale measured that of any Confederate. If, however, they marched far into alien land, Breckinridge would have to watch them. His corps, then, while an organization of size and stature to compliment him, could not be regarded as an unmixed blessing.[17]

But Early certainly rejoiced that such personnel problems as plagued Breckinridge's corps were in capable hands. He might, too, have secretly gloated that the hard-headed Gordon was subordinated to another—if so, it would have been natural, for the Georgian's opinion of Early daily seeped through a thin curtain of military courtesy.[18]

What of Robert Emmett Rodes, the VMI professor? Early wasted little concern on the youthful Virginian whose gallantry at Chancellorsville had brought him a major general's wreath. Jubal's trust easily was matched by Rodes' men, who vastly admired the blond, ramrod soldier whose black horse always roamed somewhere near the firing line.[19] Rodes needed no steadying hand and could report directly to the Commanding General. For that matter, so could Dodson Ramseur. Young he was, barely twenty-seven, but a veteran in all respects. Calm in battle and with the daring of the natural fighter, Ramseur cared for his men and they in turn cherished their boy-general who looked so fiercely forty.[20]

Infantry in hand and happily so, Early turned attention to the arm of service he most distrusted, most misunderstood, and most mishandled—the cavalry. The previous year, during his unhappy series of waltzing maneuvers through the upper end of the Valley, Early had evolved an intense dislike for the "irregulars" who seemed to cluster about John Imboden. Since his cavalry looked so poor in countering Averell, Early made the logical inference of circumstance and confusion: the cavalry was inefficient and never would be worth a good infantry regiment.[21] Anything but pleased to find at Lynchburg that

the "demoralized Imboden," as Early called him, again came
under his charge, Early had immediately concluded that all
the cavalry in Breckinridge's command were hopeless, and
Breckinridge confirmed the conclusion.[22] McCausland's gallant and most military delaying actions from Staunton to
Lynchburg were forgotten in Early's caustic fuming. Aware
that something ought to be done, but not quite certain of the
measures required, Jubal had called for help, had welcomed
General Ransom as an old infantry officer who could handle
wild troopers, and gave all cavalry problems to the West
Pointer from North Carolina. One cavalry problem only remained to be cleared up. Ransom had been reporting to Breckinridge under original orders, and now Early directed that
Ransom should report in future to Army Headquarters.

The cavalry had some added squadrons as of June 27.
Colonel Bradley T. Johnson, trusted Maryland cavalryman,
reported with the Maryland Battalion, and Jubal gave him
command of the dismounted men whose horses were coming
back to the army. Most of these men had been in the Piedmont
debacle, and were formerly Grumble Jones' brigade.[23]

Horses, their procurement and care, concerned not only
the cavalry and the supply services, but also the artillery. And
to the problems of his favorite arm, Early devoted serious attention. Arduous marching for so many days and miles had
broken down many artillery animals, and even some of the carriages and caissons were unfit to continue. Brigadier General
Long had a plan for the remainder of the campaign which
suited Early. He accepted the need to reduce the poor batteries
and determined to have Long select the best guns from his own
and Breckinridge's supply and to leave the unserviceable ones
behind as a reserve. When Long had made the selection of
good guns, fully horsed the ones selected, equipped them with
new harnesses and hardware, he reported that Nelson's, Brax-

ton's and Major William McLaughlin's batteries would go forward with the army.[24] Altogether Early counted forty cannon. Artillery for the horse soldiers amounted to three batteries, sporting ten guns.[25]

If so important a branch of the army as the artillery found it necessary to cut down because of a horse shortage, other parts of the army could not escape reduction. Adhering to General Ewell's maxim that the road to glory is not followed with much baggage, Early issued a stern order cutting down all transportation. The chief quartermaster must see that corps headquarters had only one six-horse wagon; division headquarters one four-horse wagon; brigade headquarters "including brigade, quartermaster and brigade commissary of subsistence, one four-horse wagon." For each 500 men, one four-horse wagon could carry cooking utensils. With firmness born of long experience with officers, Early proscribed lavish personal baggage.

> Regimental and company officers [read the order] must carry for themselves such underclothing as they need for the present expedition, and the remainder of their baggage with the regimental baggage wagons will be stored at such place as the chief quartermaster may direct until they can be brought to the command. The above applies equally to the battalions of artillery as to the regiments of infantry and cavalry.[26]

Without real authority to do so, Early took one final step in preparing for the next stage of his march. All the reserve forces in the Valley District were disbanded, not because they were no longer needed in the field, but because Jubal felt they would perform far more effective military service by going home and working the harvest in front of his army. And considering the bumper crops which gorged the Valley, he doubtless did the correct thing, although Secretary of War Seddon bitterly complained that he had exceeded his powers.[27] He probably had,

but strict form and military courtesy bothered Early not at all
in his circumstances. If Richmond officials objected, they
could take it up with him much later.

The last thing to do, after much deliberation, was reply
to a dispatch from General Lee. Marse Robert, who lamented
Hunter's escape, again offered discretionary instructions.[28]
Early had informed him of the thin numbers coming to his
army from Breckinridge; far fewer men than Lee had hoped.
In this unanticipated situation, did Early wish to continue with
the original plan of crossing the Potomac? Early did, and in a
detailed communique, explained to General Lee his reasons
and outlined the measures taken to lighten the army, shake it
down for hard compaigning.[29] He would move down the Valley, keeping an eye cocked toward Richmond. As much of the
harvest as possible would be sent there. Early went on to
promise that his crossing of the Potomac would hinge on approval from Lee.

Prepared as well as time and resources allowed, Jubal gave
Breckinridge orders to put Gordon's men in the road early on
June 28. Faces north, spirits high, morale restored, and with
two days rations in haversacks, the men of the Army of the
Valley marched for the enemy's country. No drill parade
swells, these veterans, no Beau Brummels of Mars. They wore
anything they could find, and most of whatever it was hung in
rags; they left a trail of blood on the road because shoes had
failed to arrive. They shambled with the gait of old soldiers
accustomed to long marches and short rations. Not all that they
had was old and worn: their rifles glinted newly, their cannon
showed recent proof marks and rumbled along the roads in
reassuring numbers. There were about 10,000 of them on foot
and maybe 4,000 more on horseback and riding the caissons.
Their assignment: threaten the heart of the Union. If their
immediate future appalled some who learned of it, most seemed

MAP
SHOWING
ROUTES AND CAMPS
OF THE
ARMY OF THE VALLEY DIST.

THE SHENANDOAH VALLEY
between Staunton
and Hagerstown

Scale in Miles
0   5   10   20   30   40

Cavalry Routes — · — · —
Infantry Routes ————
Camps △△

unconcerned; but then many were survivors of every field from the Seven Days to the Wilderness and they were long past daunting.[30]

Cavalry out still to the left, guarding approaches from the Allegheny side, Early pushed the infantry rapidly northward. Gordon's men were well in advance—they had marched at dawn, and the rest of the army pulled out of camp after noon.[31] By 9 P.M. the entire column closed on Mount Sidney, a scant ten miles from Staunton. If Early chafed at the short distance, he could take comfort from the fact that much of the army had started late and that time was always wasted following a rest —men had to be reintroduced to marching routine.

Ramseur setting the pace, the army moved early on the twenty-ninth, and as the long gray column stretched down the Valley pike, the stern eminence of Massanutten Mountain loomed on the right. Around midday the men were marching through Harrisonburg, in the heart of country where the old Valley Army had followed Stonewall to victory after smashing victory in 1862—Front Royal, Winchester, Harpers Ferry, Cross Keys, Port Republic. Every mile would bring memories to some of Early's veterans and every hill would recall skirmishes.

Leading right from Harrisonburg was the road to Cross Keys and Port Republic, and another skirting the southern tip of Massanutten to Conrad's Store in the Luray Valley. Somewhere north, no one knew just where yet, were blue-coated pickets—would new encounters prove the temper of the new Valley Army? If marching speed could be reckoned as a gauge, the new foot cavalry seemed worthy of the old; on the twenty-ninth Early's men covered about twenty-four miles and went into bivouac at nightfall near Sparta.[32]

Still no word of the enemy. Early, eager for news from the cavalry, ordered Gordon once again to lead on the morning of

June 30, and to let the pace slacken slightly—just in case
Yankee videttes lurked near the critical city of New Market.
Here would be a logical place for an enemy outpost, for New
Market guarded a strategic pass leading through Massanutten
to Luray in the valley of that name. But the Rebel vanguard
approached the town and encountered nothing save happy
Confederate citizens. Every ridge now might hide an enemy
scout, but the advance continued without incident. By camp-
ing time in the evening, the head of the column bivouacked
near Hawkinstown and the rest of the army closed near Mount
Jackson, two miles behind.[33]

Early's optimism showed clearly in a dispatch to Lee that
day:

"If you can continue to threaten Grant I hope to be able to
do something for your relief and the success of our cause
shortly. I shall lose no time." [34]

By the coolish, damp evening of the first of July, Early's van
pitched camp near Strasburg, and the whole army concentrated
around Fisher's Hill. Still the enemy did not appear, and
cavalry reports coming from the left brought no alarms or
worries. Now that Strasburg lay in his grasp, Early could
count on having achieved one strategic victory already: he
had cleared the upper Shenandoah; all the rich harvest of the
rolling, fertile hills south of Strasburg was safe; and the yield
of Luray, too, could be sent to Rebel depots. Another thing:
when he reached Strasburg, Early had cleared the shadow of
Massanutten and removed any nagging threat from beyond.
His right now stretched to the Blue Ridge, and he counted on
loyal citizens and ranging scouts of Major John Mosby to
warn of impending trouble from that quarter. He would not
linger at Strasburg, but would stick to the Valley pike and press
forward as fast as the bleeding feet of his men allowed.

They moved rapidly on the second; Gordon's men setting

the stride. Early and staff mounted soon that Saturday morning
and trotted ahead of the infantry. At Middletown, five miles
out of Strasburg, they halted for breakfast while the infantry
trudged past. By 11 A.M., July 2, the general and his entourage
rode into Winchester. What a welcome awaited them! Time
and again Confederates commented on the fanatical loyalty of
this Valley town—always it had been one of Stonewall's favor-
ites. Though often the pawns of war, often in the grips of the
enemy, the townspeople never wavered in their steadfast devotion to the gray; and each time the ragged boys from Lee
marched into Winchester, the town went mad. Shouting citizens lined the streets, waved flags, and offered some of their
scant larder to their redeemers. This warm Saturday morning
proved no exception. Early's arrival amounted almost to a
triumph, and Headquarters, Army of the Valley, lacked for no
comforts the citizens could provide.[35]

At Winchester Early began to get information on Federal
activities. Reports indicated that General Franz Sigel, the
goat of New Market, had a considerable force at Martinsburg,
little more than forty miles north on a direct road for Hagerstown, Maryland. At Martinsburg, Sigel held a station on the
Baltimore and Ohio Railroad and a road hub for the lower
Valley. But in some ways his position was poor. Should he be
attacked, he could be cut off from roads leading toward help
at Harpers Ferry, and would have to fall back across the
Potomac. Should this happen, Harpers Ferry might easily fall
to Early, since its garrison could not cope with the Valley
Army. Early's concern now was to exploit the enemy's weak
strategic position swiftly and effectively.

General Lee was right in judging that one of Jubal's greatest
assets was his willingness to fight. Early plotted to hit Sigel
hard, trap him, smash him, capture the remnants. Ridding himself of Sigel would fit in with Early's new plans—plans made

upon receipt of an important communication from Lee. In this dispatch, Lee urged Jubal to remain in the lower Valley until "everything was in readiness" to cross into Maryland. The Commanding General wished Early to tear up a good portion of the B&O track and wreck as much of the Chesapeake & Ohio Canal as possible before launching his incursion into enemy country; if done well, the breaks in these main arteries of Yankee travel would isolate bluecoated troops operating west of Harpers Ferry and would interrupt Federal arrangements to reinforce the Valley or Washington. Lee doubtless knew, too, that Early's provisions were low and that should he move eastward and attempt a crossing of the Potomac nearer Washington, he would enter land stripped of forage and grain. Lee's caveat had really been unnecessary: Jubal had already recognized the logistical problems which crossing the Blue Ridge would entail and decided to stay within the confines of the Shenandoah.

> My provisions [he later recalled] were nearly exhausted and if I had moved through Loudon, it would have been necessary for me to halt and thresh wheat and have it ground, as neither bread nor flour could be otherwise obtained; which would have caused much greater delay than was required on the other route, where we could take provisions from the enemy.[36]

With these strategic and logistical considerations in mind, Early summoned John McCausland to headquarters in Winchester. Plug of tobacco churning furiously, as it inevitably did when Jube was exercised, he gave his cavalry leader exciting orders. Go, said the grizzled commanding general, through the Allegheny Mountains into Black Creek Valley, gallop northward to the mouth of the stream, burn the B&O bridge, and range eastward along the tracks to North Mountain Depot. At that point, leave the rail line and strike for the highway leading from Martinsburg to the Potomac. Hold that road, hold it until reinforced or ordered away! Move at once, and avoid the usual delays of horse soldiers! A smart salute, hurried adieus, and McCausland joined his troopers. After sundown, a long line of horsemen filed quietly from the Rebel camps, and trotted northwestward. If the infantry wondered at their direction, no immediate explanation came from Old Jube.

The old man worried through the rest of his plan: on the morning of the third, reliable Bradley Johnson, one of the sounder cavalrymen, must take his brigade north toward Smithfield and Leetown, "cross the railroad at Kearneysville, east of Martinsburg, and unite with McCausland at Hainesville," on the road from Martinsburg to the Potomac. The junction of these two forces would cut off Sigel's retreat from Martinsburg. To prod Sigel into the trap was the job of the infantry. Breckinridge received orders to march directly for the enemy at Martinsburg, and press back any Federals encountered. Jubal, himself, would lead Rodes and Ramseur over Bradley Johnson's route to Leetown; a heavy infantry force at Leetown ought to prevent Sigel's escape toward Harpers Ferry and eliminate his choice of retreat routes. Here was strategy reminiscent of Stonewall's at Front Royal. Force the enemy to do exactly what the strategist desired, and force him to do it at the utmost disadvantage. Jubal had learned a great deal from his old mentor. Now, if he could achieve proper coordination, he might win a victory to rank with some of Jackson's!

Sunday dawned clear and hot.[37] With the first streaks of light Early could see his infantry already shambling toward Martinsburg. At Brucetown, some seven miles up the road, Breckinridge's and Gordon's divisions took the left fork and continued on toward Martinsburg, while Rodes and Ramseur, with

Jubal in their lead, took the right fork toward Leetown. Despite the heat and hard sweating, all seemed well, and Early had little worry about the outcome of his plan.

But he had reckoned without Sigel, or rather without Sigel's crumbling nerves. Instead of waiting until the situation near Martinsburg developed, Sigel bolted on first information that Rebels were coming. This intelligence came shortly after 6 A.M. from Sigel's left, where Colonel James Mulligan with a small part of the Twenty-third Illinois ran into Bradley Johnson's troopers in the vicinity of Leetown. Mulligan put up a stubborn fight, and was spurred to great efforts by orders from Sigel to fall back slowly toward Kearneysville, thence to Shepherdstown. Sigel wanted him to buy time to concentrate the Union forces and to get most of the depot stores out of Martinsburg.[38]

Sigel's determination for Mulligan was admirable, but not matched by his own. While the Twenty-third Illinois struggled to hold a Federal road of retreat, word arrived at Sigel's harried headquarters of Breckinridge's columns moving up from Winchester. Directing some of the vast supplies stored at Martinsburg to be loaded on railroad cars and some on wagons, Sigel sent the trains eastward toward Shepherdstown on the Potomac. As soon as his wagons cleared the town, Sigel evacuated it [39] and followed the train. But in the haste and confusion of getting out, Federal quartermasters had been unable to remove all the stores; large warehouses remained untouched.

The center of operations now shifted to the road leading eastward to Shepherdstown. On this road struggled the long Yankee wagon train; on it, too, the main force of the enemy marched to cross into Maryland and out of Jubal's clutches. The issue rested with Bradley Johnson and Mulligan. Sigel had taken the road Early had hoped to cut with Johnson's force, but Johnson had been unable to reach it as rapidly as desired. He must break Mulligan and drive him into the wagons. On the other side, Mulligan must hold out, contesting each inch of ground, until the wagons cleared his rear. To assist him, Sigel detached as much of his small force (not over 5,000) as he could spare.

Late in the afternoon Sigel's situation approached ruin. Breckinridge and Gordon had marched into Martinsburg, through it, and were moving out on the Shepherdstown road. Robert Ransom had reached Johnson's force, surveyed the action against Mulligan, and plotted how to get past the enemy and into the wagons. Sigel marched desperately along the road, and hoped the reinforcements he sent the Twenty-third Illinois would stave off disaster.

As it turned out, they did. Mulligan, with 1,000 dismounted troopers to help him, plus two guns and 1,500 cavalry, stopped Johnson and launched a limited counterattack. Suddenly checked and struck a hard blow by strong enemy forces, Johnson's front broke and he had to retreat rapidly toward Leetown —where he hoped to find Early and some infantry support. He found infantry alright, but by the time he reached Leetown's outskirts Ramseur's veterans were in camp, resting from a fiercely hot twenty-four-mile march. The mere presence of Rebel infantry, however, proved enough to stop Mulligan's offensive; he wanted no general fight, just time to cover the wagons. He withdrew without trouble. Irate that he could inflict no punishment on the retiring enemy, Early nonetheless realized that after so stern a day's effort he could expect no more from the weary foot soldiers. He established headquarters near Ramseur's camps and slept, while Sigel fled to safety across the Potomac.[40]

Up to now the whole campaign had been something of a disappointment. Although Hunter had been pushed out of the

Shenandoah, Lee had already expressed Early's own frustration in a sad letter to President Davis:

> General Hunter has escaped Early. . . . Although his expedition has been partially interrupted, I fear he has not been much punished, except by the demoralization of his troops and the loss of some artillery.[41]

And now Sigel had escaped Early and had not been "much punished" except by the loss of considerable amounts of supplies. Two chances to wreck enemy armies; two chances missed. What was wrong? Was the Army of the Valley too weak for its mission; were its officers unable to coordinate activities; or was the commanding general to blame? In military usage, of course, Early was to blame, if blame could be justly assessed. As Early pondered missed chances, however, he wasted no time on self-recriminations. He would do his best to plan more carefully in the immediate future, and he would do his best to mystify the already confused enemy. It might be possible to turn a partial frustration into a strategic success if Sigel's fears were exploited.

Early stayed with his right wing, and made his plans from the vicinity of Leetown and Halltown. And while he cogitated once again, some of his men enjoyed a moment of fantastic debauchery.

The moment came to Breckinridge's corps, and especially to the fortunate men of Gordon's division. These were the ones who had the pleasure of occupying Martinsburg and of finding the bulging warehouses. Not only were the warehouses full, but also the depot and the express office offered bumper crops of packages for the taking. Sigel's army had been preparing for a gala Fourth of July celebration, and all sorts of delicacies from Yankee kitchens had been sent to them. Some of Gordon's veterans must have conjured up a vision of another great

gorging, a day still fresh in the minds of any who had been at
Manassas Junction with Stonewall in August, 1862. Gordon,
of course, saw the danger to discipline inherent in these tempta-
tions and placed a guard around all the storehouses. A sound
scheme, but hardly a deterrent to Rebel scavengers—old hands
at the art. Let one of the most experienced tell of his success in
cracking the defenses at the express office:

> The express office was put in charge of a quartermaster who
> was an old friend of mine. At night I went there and inquired
> of the guard for him and he let me into the building. He was
> very glad to see me, as he had only one man to help him get
> these articles in shape, and asked me to help him; this I con-
> sented to do, if he would give me a barrel of cakes. He said
> 'all right.' I found one and carried it out and turned it over
> to my company. Returning, I went to work with a will, but
> with so many good things in sight, and others we knew were
> in the boxes, I was compelled to say to my friend that I must
> have something to eat before I could work any more, and
> added, 'I hadn't "nary" mouthful for three days.' I looked over
> some of the boxes and choosing one, opened it, and found it
> filled with cakes, oranges, bananas, lemons, etc., and a bottle
> of wine. I got a chair, as the soldiers said 'a sure enough chair,'
> and sat down to my box and ate, and ate, until I could eat no
> more. Then I went to work again with renewed energy. . . .
> I opened [a] trunk. In it was a magnificent saddle and a lot of
> clothing, which I gave to the quartermaster, a fine pair of
> boots, a gold pen, a lot of writing paper, and a plum cake
> which I 'confiscated,' the boots fitting me to a T. When my feet
> were healed so that I could wear them, I wore them until I
> went home. I joined my company, who were profuse in their
> thanks for the cakes, and soon fell asleep,—dreaming of little
> cakes, big cakes, and a mountain made of cakes.[42]

Company F, Twenty-first Virginia Infantry, came out far
ahead of the rest of the corps as a result of John Worsham's
enterprise, but the whole command did fairly well. On the

morning of the fourth, Breckinridge withheld marching orders
until much of the richness of Martinsburg had been shared by
the grayclads.[43]

The remainder of the army, green with envy at Breckinridge's men, faced a hard day's activity. Early and staff moved
at daylight, breakfasted at Major Hawks' hospitable home,[44]
and pushed ahead of the infantry to Charlestown, then on to
Halltown where Federal skirmishers were encountered. At
Halltown, Ramseur's and Rodes men were in easy distance of
Harpers Ferry and Early ordered them forward as fast as the
enemy retired—which proved to be fast indeed. By 9 A.M.
Bolivar Heights, that long ridge of hills guarding the southwestern approaches to Harpers Ferry, were in sight and Ramseur filed to the left to take possession of the B&O tracks. Rodes
deployed on the Charlestown road and aligned straight for the
hills. When the divisions were arranged, Early's right rested
on the Shenandoah and his front curved in a concave line
around to the Potomac, where Ramseur's left elements stood
guard. Forward, Jubal ordered, and steady advance gained the
crest of Bolivar Heights without much fighting; Federal defenders retired to an inner line of works. Now Early could
survey the main Union positions. As he swept the town of
Harpers Ferry and environs with his glasses, he could scarcely
have been encouraged.

Harpers Ferry lay on a triangular spit of land formed by the
Shenandoah River running in from the south and the Potomac
running down from the west. The land approaches from the
southwest were guarded by several ridges of hills, the most
prominent being Bolivar Heights. But as Early's glasses turned
back and forth, the real strengths of Harpers Ferry stood
clearly in view. In front of his men on Bolivar ran a secondary
line of lesser hills which had been turned into an emergency
earth work barring immediate entry to the town. Across the

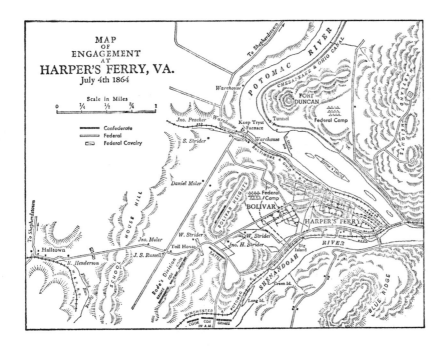

MAP
OF
ENGAGEMENT
AT
HARPER'S FERRY, VA.
July 4th 1864

rock-flecked Potomac, and rising virtually out of the river, loomed the craggy eminence called Maryland Heights. Commanding all the terrain for miles, this peak bristled with Union batteries, and their big guns glinted in the clear sunlight. Sweeping toward the right with his glasses, Early caught sight of another peak of slightly less majesty, this one on the Rebel side of the Potomac and across the Shenandoah. Loudon Heights had figured prominently in Stonewall's artillery siege of Harpers Ferry in September, 1862, and Early knew of the lethal work done by Jackson's guns posted east of the Shenandoah. The huge enemy cannon on Maryland Heights—they looked like 100-pounders—were enough to deter Jubal from an attack, but should the enemy have guns on Loudon, he might have to fall back to avoid a searing crossfire. Fortunately the rocky hilltop seemed bare, the green scrub growth undisturbed by engines of war. But Federal positions on Maryland Heights dominated Harpers Ferry, and made any thought of attack absurd. Jubal would have to think on the situation and see what his opponent, General Max Weber at Harpers Ferry, decided to do.

Once determined to wait, Early began his concentration of infantry. Ramseur and Rodes, of course, were in hand. Breckinridge's corps, after its gustatory exercises, had burned the bridges at Martinsburg, moved down the B&O through Kearneysville and camped late in the day at Duffield's Depot, five miles from Early's lines at Harpers Ferry. With Sigel north of the Potomac, Early gave full attention to Weber and to the Federal units still south of the river, scattered in small parties from Harpers Ferry well into West Virginia. The cavalry received orders to attack as many of the bridgehead guards as possible in order to create the impression of a huge Confederate force operating in the lower Valley. And despite Early's low opinion of him, John Imboden, under Ransom's orders, did a thorough job of pestering assorted Union outposts, as far up-river as Sir John's Run. Lieutenant Colonel John Mosby, voluntarily cooperating with Early, confused the Federals thoroughly at Point of Rocks. As Kyd Douglas observed, Jubal "spread his little army, like a fan." [45] Even if he spread it too thin, the enemy was in no condition to estimate his real strength.

Continued shelling and the report of Breckinridge's approach from Martinsburg shattered General Weber's resolution during the afternoon of the fourth. Several times avowing his determination to hold Harpers Ferry at all costs and to the last extremity, he confessed to General Henry Halleck, Federal Chief of Staff, that he must evacuate the town during the night —if no help arrived. Through the late part of the afternoon, Weber watched the evacuation of most of his stores across the Potomac, and at nightfall, having heard nothing from Sigel or anyone else, he fell back to Maryland Heights with his entire garrison.

Jubal and his staff rode to Bolivar Heights in the early hours of Tuesday morning, saw the empty works and strangely quiet town. A quick sweep of the Heights confirmed the fact: they were heavily reinforced; Weber obviously had decided to hold them. The glance convinced Jubal that he could not occupy the town, however; enemy cannon would blast his men out as soon as they moved in. He directed Ramseur and Rodes to demonstrate, hold Bolivar Heights, and police the town with skirmishers—a thin curtain of Confederates probably would not draw fire. [46]

Balked at Harpers Ferry, cut off from easy access to the Washington pike, Early decided to take the initiative in another sector. If he had to wait for supplies, he could harass the enemy as much as possible while waiting, and continue the game of numbers-guessing he had begun. And while engaged

in this elaborate ruse, he would threaten Weber and worry
Sigel. Relatively easy in the knowledge that McCausland pa-
trolled his left and rear, and that Mosby had sealed off Union
communications with Washington,[47] Early gave Breckinridge
the most daring orders of a fairly daring career: Go across the
Potomac, shoes or no shoes! Put Gordon in the road near Duffield's Depot and push him toward Boteler's Ford—a ford
famed in the annals of the Second Corps.[48]

As soon as the entire disposition of his troops had been
reviewed, Early climbed into the saddle and trotted to Halltown, thence to Leetown where he turned right into the road
for Shepherdstown and the Potomac. Ramseur and Rodes had
orders to go into Harpers Ferry after dark and capture lost
Yankee loot and then to leave a brigade behind to amuse the
bluecoats. That done, they could cross the river.

Up from the South the infantry marched, lazy swirls of dust
coasting above the columns. Finally the tattered gray men saw
the old ford again, the racing river, the green banks of Maryland. Many of them had been over that crossing several times;
twice had Lee's whole army been thrown into Maryland only
to come back thinned in ranks and shattered in hopes. Invasion
days before had been happy, frolicsome occasions; bands
played, citizens cheered, banners flapped in favorable Confederate zephyrs. But the war had changed in tone and time;
troops now conserved enthusiasm for food and tiny comforts,
citizens now were calloused to war's tide. No bands played
"Maryland, My Maryland." Soldiers marched to the river and
each man sought his own best way to cross the rocky ford *sans*
footgear. Private John Worsham pretty well summed up the
sentiments of the invaders that day:

> I walked into the water and commenced to ford. About one-
> third of the way the bottom of the river was covered with large
> round stones, then a smooth and level bed of granite which

extended nearly to the opposite bank. I got along very well
until I reached the level granite bottom, which was covered
with minute shells, adhering to the granite, so very sharp that
they stuck into my feet at every step. I walked on them until I
thought I could not take another step, stopped, but could not
keep my feet still,—thought of sitting down, but the water was
just deep enough to cover my mouth and nose if I had sat
down. I thought I would turn back, but I saw it was just as
far back as to the other side. Tears actually came into my eyes.
I was never in as much torture for the same length of time in
my life. Finally I got over, with the resolve never to ford there
again without shoes.[49]

Now on Yankee ground, Gordon's men were marched
rapidly southeastward and camped for the night near Antietam
Furnace. They would be in position to trouble the Federals on
Maryland Heights in the morning; Early had not quite aban-
doned hope of maneuvering the enemy off the high ground.
General John Vaughn took Breckinridge's other division into
Sharpsburg and camped around the battle scarred town.[50]
Jubal himself enjoyed a lark with some of the troops near
Antietam Furnace; he helped burn several canal boats on the
C&O, but came back to the Virginia shore for the night. Not
until morning of Wednesday, July 6, did he move Headquarters, Army of the Valley, officially north of the border.[51]
When, at last, he did bring all the army over, Kyd Douglas
marveled at Jubal's nerve. To invade the North with so few,
he thought, "was a desperate thing to do. . . . It was so reckless that historians are still examining figures to see if it can
be possible. Jackson being dead, it is safe to say no other
General in either army would have attempted it against such
odds." [52] But odds were relative, and Early gambled that the
enemy counted too heavily on them. Audacity proved its own
reward.

FATEFUL HOURS ON A RIVER

WEDNESDAY, JULY 6, dawned clear and warm. More of Early's infantry came up and splashed across the river. With them rode the commanding general. Kyd Douglas rounded up Early, Breckinridge, Gordon, and friend Ramseur, and extended an invitation to visit his father's house. Close to Sharpsburg, the Douglas home had a reputation as one of southern Maryland's most hospitable, and the generals gladly accepted. The senior Douglas, who had suffered no little as the father of a noted Rebel, greeted the visitors graciously, and after a brief call the group rode out to view the famed battlefield.[1] Curious how a scant two years could change a countryside; the main landmarks were still there—Burnside's Bridge, the cemetery near the Boonsboro Pike where Longstreet's artillery had stood almost alone against a whole Yankee corps, the ridge along the Antietam where Harvey Hill had done desperate battle and where so many had died in the Bloody Lane. To the left, Early could see again the diminutive Dunkard Church—the memories it brought back! On a September morn two years ago he had waked to the roar of cannon from beyond McClellan's lines, had heard the awful crash of Union volleys and then had received a chilling order from Stonewall Jackson: move with all the men at hand to hold what once had been the Confederate front. And through one of the longest days in the recall of the army, Early's men had fiercely hurled back Hooker's advancing corps. The fields were quiet now, the corn golden and tall where once it had been sheared by bullets and stained red with blood. Over the battlefield in the summer sun, the silent rage of past combat flooded into the memory of those who had been tested here.

But not all of war could be measured in stirring moments. Now that he commanded an army, Early experienced more than ever before the dull drudgery of administrative detail, the housekeeping chores necessary to the daily life of a field force. While he thought of old battles and looked eastward to South Mountain and Maryland Heights and chafed to get beyond the mountains on the most important campaign of his life, matters of logistics forced him to hold back his eagerness. Shoes had yet to come from the south; forage and rations were scarce and would have to be procured by parties of foragers and commissaries who were dispatched into the bountiful countryside with Confederate money and certificates of impressment. Food and provender would be taken legally and with proper offer of payment in either Confederate paper or certificates. Early would tolerate no heavy-handed use of the power of commandeering—he was already agitated about the face the army was presenting to Maryland and the world.

In the enemy's country the Confederate Army had always maintained strict discipline. A year earlier, when Lee's columns streamed into Pennsylvania, the Rebs had done almost no marauding, pillage had been held to a surprising minimum, and discipline had been excellent. But news had reached Jubal of the sacking of the warehouses in Martinsburg, and he worried lest this incident forecast a serious decline in discipline and morale. Breckinridge had commanded at Martinsburg, and he received a tactful but unmistakable rebuke from Early, who published a General Order warning all the troops that any depredations would be "summarily punished." [2]

There was one other disturbing indication of decaying morale, of crumbling command. Early had directed John Imboden to take his cavalry and operate in the South Branch Valley. Imboden had done reasonably well during the operations around Martinsburg, and had then been sent back to work diligently at wrecking the B&O in the South Branch. Early knew that if the tracks were properly damaged, Hunter would probably not be able to get back into the theater of war in time to be a problem. Imboden had begun well enough, apparently, but his force had gone to pieces when he fell sick. The result: little damage to the enemy's prime route of communication with the west. Early would have to rely on Hunter's innate timidity; nothing else protected the Confederate rear. [3]

While Early worked to accumulate supplies and waited on the truant shoes, he kept an active front against Maryland Heights. Gordon's men, already on the road toward the Heights, were sent further on and encouraged to find the extent of enemy defenses. Some of Sigel's and Weber's skirmishers were found, and brisk contact drove them back into some fairly formidable works guarding the approaches to the Heights. Apparently the two commands had united and the Federals intended to hold the eminence with determination.

As soon as Gordon's men occupied Yankee attention, wrecking parties went to work on the C&O canal aqueduct, hacked at the locks and destroyed canal boats. Early, meantime, continued his elaborate scheme of enemy befuddlement. His troopers received orders to ride in all directions and stir up trouble, be seen at several points simultaneously, and create the illusion of large masses. John McCausland's orders were

explicit enough: go to Hagerstown and levy a contribution.
Hagerstown was a fairly sizeable community, and Jubal esti-
mated that the populace could stand an assessment of
$200,000. But McCausland's luck held bad—rarely could he
do anything right for Early. When he got the order, he missed
a digit, and demanded a contribution from the city officials of
only $20,000.⁴ But the error could be forgiven, since the
desired impression of strength began to spread. Reports flooded
into Baltimore and Washington of Rebels thundering all over
Maryland and even into Pennsylvania. Worry began to settle
heavily on the United States War Department. And at headquarters of the United States Middle Department in Baltimore,
worry was about to produce brave, if hasty, action.

During the hot afternoon of the sixth, Early pondered future
plans at headquarters in a shady orchard near Sharpsburg.
Several possibilities were worth considering. He could attempt
to turn the southern tip of Maryland Heights; he could storm
the Heights and drive the defenders ahead of him toward
Washington; he could avoid battle by moving a little farther
north and crossing South Mountain through the passes used
during the 1862 invasion.

Early liked to fight, and in almost any other circumstances
would have directed that Sigel's and Weber's Yanks be thrown
off their hill. But the mantle of responsibility settled on him,
and he knew he must again put prudence above sport. The
idea was confirmed that day.

Sometime in the afternoon a courier dashed into the headquarters camp, reined up, and swung from his saddle. Hurry-
ing to Early, he saluted smartly, and Jubal warmly welcomed
General Lee's young son, Robert.⁵ If Robert carried a dispatch,
it must be vital, indeed. So it was, and it was also mysterious.

There would be an attempt to free the prisoners at Point
Lookout, below Baltimore, the dispatch read, and Early should

make arrangements to cooperate with this effort by detaching some cavalry in the direction of Baltimore to create a diversion and to join in the liberation if needed. Details were lacking, and a query to Robert brought assurance that he himself knew nothing of the scheme, and that his father knew no more than the bare outline. Early would have to rely on enemy sources for indications of success, and on his cavalry for any communication from Confederate sympathizers who were aiding some daring Southern naval officers in the plan. Scant as were details, Early did not have to be told the importance of the scheme: there were some 18,000 Confederates in the Point Lookout prison, and if set free they not only would constitute a whole army corps for Lee, but also might give Early enough strength to do mortal damage to the Union. Any fleeting thoughts of smashing up Maryland Heights vanished, and Early went to his field desk to draft a reply for Robert to carry to his father.

General Lee must have been encouraged at the judicious tone his independent subordinate took. Early recounted his problem in strategy, explained he had planned to cross the river at Harpers Ferry, but that Federal occupation of Maryland Heights had deprived him of easy ingress into the vicinity of Frederick and Washington. Now, with the news of the clandestine operations planned at Point Lookout, he would do what he felt all along he must—cross the mountains via the passes used two years before. Once through the passes, he would endeavor to find what the enemy plotted for him and would send some cavalry to cooperate with any program developing near Point Lookout. Such caution showed that Early had been learning under the test of independent command, but Lee still kept a close eye on him. He urged Early to get Federal papers; they were excellent sources of intelligence. He urged him, too, to watch toward the west for the

approach of Hunter, whom the entire North counted on to
catch the Army of the Valley. With Early's basic plan he had
no quarrel—approved it in a letter to the President [6]—but
doubtless felt that a modicum of supervision would be wise.

If Early chafed at suggestions from Lee, he gave no sign.
His preparations went ahead rapidly, and when the sorely
needed shoes arrived on the seventh, he was ready.

At an early hour that Thursday morning, Gordon's men
renewed pressure on the Federals at the Heights and drove
them to one of their stronger forts. Early watched the fighting
with critical eye and waited for word from other units. Breckinridge with Rodes' division reported from Pleasant Valley,
near Rohrersville, and Ramseur's men, according to one report,
were recovering from spiked lemon punch near Sharpsburg.[7]
Ransom's cavalry received orders to probe the passes through
South Mountain. Some of his units had been picketing the
passes during the past day [8] and the crest was in Confederate
hands. East of Crampton's and Boonsboro Gaps lay a beautiful
valley, guarded on its eastern edge by Catoctin Mountain.
Bradley Johnson's cavalry, en route to Catoctin Pass, trotted
through the sleepy hamlet of Middletown about 10 A.M., when
the sudden, sharp report of a cannon brought them to a halt.
On one of the hills which rolled across the valley Johnson
spotted a line of blue cavalry, and the column was bearing
down on the Confederates. Before anyone could get set, the
Eighth Illinois rode into the Rebs and Lieutenant Colonel
David Clendenin's disciplined troopers swept the field. Johnson's men—surprised, and momentarily routed—retired for
almost a half mile before reinforcements steadied them, and
artillery support came up. Fighting dismounted in line of battle,
they began to push Clendenin back, prodded his retreat and
finally shoved him into Catoctin Pass.[9]

Johnson brought up more men and pressed on. He noted

that Clendenin had deployed in a line to cover the pass, but that there were too few bluecoats to prevent flanking. Instantly he ordered some 250 troopers forward as skirmishers to occupy the Union front. To the right and left went squadrons with orders to ride around Clendenin's flanks and roll him up. Clendenin saw the threats and knew he could not hold. By about 11 A.M. he gave up Catoctin Pass and retired on Frederick, Maryland.[10]

Johnson's men followed to the crest of the Pass, and glimpsed a vista to remember. The mountain fell away gently, and almost at the edge of the blue-green, lushly shrubbed foothills lay Frederick. In the clear sunshine, its red bricks and carefully whitened frames shimmered; it had that ordered look of Maryland. Around it wheat waved lazily in the summer breeze, an occasional church spire loomed, and red barns marked the farmhouses. An aura of peace and plenty covered the Frederick vale, an aura disturbed only by a line of blue infantry in the suburbs and by several ugly black cannon trained toward the mountain.[11]

Johnson faced two new tasks. Early, of course, had to be informed that the enemy had been met—Ransom and the commanding general wanted to know when and where the enemy waited, and in what strength. The question of strength posed Johnson's second task: develop the enemy, engage him strongly enough to make him expose his main force on the field.

Obviously there were infantry in Frederick, and to find out the size of the detachment would take some doing. Apparently the foot soldiers were supported by a field battery, and perhaps by still more artillery. No cavalry charge on the outskirts of Frederick would do the job. Johnson waited until he could bring up support himself, then decided to deploy a dismounted line. All of this took time—he had to survey the field, check his ammunition, bring up guns, work his men into position.

Noon came and went, the sun beat down from a clear sky, and
both sides sweated through the tense period of shifting and
reshifting as each commander flexed his command for battle.
At 4 P.M. Johnson's three field pieces opened fire, and his
skirmishers snaked through the stands of wheat toward the
Federals. The sharp pop-popping of skirmish fire began, rose
in volume, and became a high-pitched rattle as the main lines
came to grips.

No sooner did the main lines make contact than Johnson
saw he had troubles aplenty. Not only was the Federal ordnance good, but also the infantry. Steady these bluecoats were,
some Maryland units mixed with the Eighth Illinois Cavalry,
under resolute officers, and many armed with deadly Sharp's
carbines.[12] But Bradley Johnson knew the ground—Frederick
was home to him. He sized up the tactical situation when he
discovered that the Yankees had as many guns on the line as
he did and that they would fight. If he pressed the enemy
straight on—there looked to be about a thousand of them in
front of him—he might at the same time throw a column south
toward the Georgetown pike, another by the reservoir road
into the north end of town, rush in behind the defenders and
capture the lot.

With this plan in mind, he began shifting slightly to his right
as the afternoon dragged on, and directed his front line to
keep up a steady volume of fire. By six in the evening, Johnson's Rebels were far enough toward the south of Frederick to
threaten the Federal left flank. As the Yankees tried to change
front a little to meet the threat, it came clear that some of
the starch had gone out of them. The pitch of enemy musket
and carbine fire slackened considerably. Apparently their guns
were low on ammunition, for heavy shelling ceased and only
an occasional round burst in the Confederate lines.[13]

At this critical moment, General Robert Ransom took a hand

in the battle. When his superior reached the field, Johnson outlined his plan for flanking both ends of the enemy front. To Ransom's cautious query about chances of enemy resistance, Johnson replied that the enemy's entire strength already had been committed to the front; flanking parties should encounter no serious barriers. The temper of the citizens, their constant offers of information to an old friend, convinced Johnson of the feasibility of his simple and effective scheme. Ransom begged to doubt, mulled the problem awhile, and at length concluded that Johnson's optimism could not be justified. He seemed infatuated with getting back to old stomping grounds—judgment might have yielded to nostalgia. Call off the attack, said the major general, fall back to Catoctin Mountain. Enough already had been gleaned from the day's skirmishing: the enemy blocked the roads toward Baltimore and Washington, but apparently not in overwhelming numbers. Nor were the bluecoats presently engaged attached to any of the real veteran regiments of the Union armies. Learning this fact alone justified the day's work, and also justified calling a halt to combat. General Early would be interested to know that home brigades were in front, that none of Grant's men had reached the theater.

Johnson, naturally enough, was disgusted. Just as his trap had been ready to spring, all his men in position, he had to call off the whole enterprise. What galled him most was the fact that as his men backed up toward the mountain, Federal energy revived and the enemy moved out to speed the pace of Southern retreat. The Yanks appeared to think they had beaten Johnson, and this he resented.

At least one Federal thought a northern victory had been won. From his temporary headquarters at Moncacy Junction, about three miles southeast of Frederick, Major General Lew Wallace had listened anxiously during the day. Wind and rolling hills played havoc with acoustics, and as the sound of firing rose and fell, so the general's hopes. Wallace was by nature optimistic—a fact belied by his long, thin face, his drooping moustache and sad eyes. A professional soldier every inch of his frame, this tall gaunt Indianan had nonetheless an acute sense of drama, an apperception of history. While Early skirmished around Harpers Ferry, Wallace had been discharging the rather sedentary duties of commander of the U.S. Army's Middle Department. Headquarters were in Baltimore, which offered some small compensation for absence from the field. Wallace remembered earlier days of battle in the west, and though he made himself a good department manager, he could generate no love for the position. Rumors of Rebel activity around the Ferry flurried in the newspapers, but since these activities lay outside the confines of his geographical charge, he noted them without excitement. Then Sigel crossed into Maryland, apparently dazed and uncertain about Rebel numbers; Weber abandoned the bridges at the Ferry and retired to the protection of Maryland Heights; reports came from places like Cumberland, that hordes of Southern horsemen were roaming above the Potomac.

Wallace's sixth sense went to work. If, he reasoned, the Rebs had indeed crossed into Maryland, this meant that they were unusually reckless or strong enough to dare opposition. If they were strong, then they might be thinking of a dash at Washington. As he thought about the possible consequence of a move on the capital, "they grouped themselves into a kind of horrible schedule." [14] There, ready for the torch, was the Navy Yard; there, too, the Treasury with millions in negotiable bonds and currency; and above all there were warehouses brimming with necessities for the Army of the Potomac. If the Quartermaster Department were to lose its six-acre depot (where $11 million worth of supplies, extensive shops and

machinery were presently housed, and where 32,000 horses
and 15,000 mules could be handled at one time),[15] if the ordnance depots, the medical depots, and warehouses of food were
lost to the Rebels, "the war must halt, if not stop for good
and all." [16] So horrible a prospect demanded instant action.

At midnight of July 4–5, Wallace and a single staff officer
made their quiet way to the depot and swung aboard a waiting
engine. Having left details of defending Baltimore, of arming
volunteers, and of calling out Union Leagues to subordinates
authorized to sign for him, Wallace turned attention to his
destination. He decided that Monocacy Junction would be the
best place for an observation post; the Junction was in his
department, and it covered main roads to Baltimore and
Washington. But he had to keep his departure as quiet as
possible. General Henry Halleck, sober Chief-of-Staff of the
U.S. Army, had been trying to pin some breach of regulations
on Wallace for many months, and departure from Baltimore
without orders "might be turned to my [Wallace's] serious
disadvantage." [17] If, after arrival at the Junction, he could
find out the strength of the enemy and provide reliable information for Grant, then he would make his location known in
Washington.

Meantime he would scrape together all the piecemeal forces
in the area and prepare to find the Rebels. By the seventh he
had picked up stray infantry units from Baltimore, a few
mounted man, and had commandeered the Eighth Illinois
Cavalry. Clendenin had been trying to develop Confederate
numbers on orders from General Christopher C. Augur, commanding the Department of Washington, but readily obeyed
orders from Wallace. Altogether Wallace counted not more
than 2,300 men. But this appeared a large enough force to
reconnoiter the territory west of Frederick and to probe the
mountains. With that in mind, he had dispatched the Eighth

Illinois on an expedition with an intent which coincided exactly with that of Bradley Johnson's—reconnaissance in force toward Catoctin Pass.[18]

When Clendenin and Johnson had engaged at 10 A.M. on the seventh, the sound carried clearly to Wallace. He waited near a blockhouse guarding the railroad bridge at Monocacy. As more men arrived by rail, he hurried them on to Frederick, and his efforts provided the infantry support which awaited Clendenin as he fell back from Catoctin Pass. Through the afternoon Wallace heard the firing, and knew the peculiar anxiety of a soldier who could not go to the sound of battle. When, in the late afternoon, the fire faded around Frederick, Wallace received word that Federal ammunition was running low, that Johnson's grayclads were threatening the Union left, and that the town would probably fall. Reinforcements were urgently needed. There were some men at the Junction, but Wallace knew he dare not send them forward—if they went, the vital bridges over the Monocacy River would be bare of defenders.

Instead of sending reinforcements, he sent to subordinates in Frederick news which had reached him not long before:

> I have a telegram announcing veterans from Grant landing at Baltimore, and they will be up some time tonight. . . . The fellows fighting you are only dismounted cavalry, and you can whip them. Try a charge. . . .[19]

At about the time this message reached the frazzled defenders of Frederick, firing increased and the Rebels retired. Wallace concluded, logically enough, that his word of reinforcement had won the day. Elated, convinced that with help he could hold the strategic Junction, he announced "the best little battle of the war" to Baltimore, and reported victory to Halleck. The fighting, he thought, had just begun, and made ready for July 8—a day which might bring definite intelligence about Rebel strength.

Beyond South Mountain, at headquarters still in the Sharpsburg orchard, Early received a report of the cavalry action, paid it small attention. Ransom's report indicated he had come upon a local force which would offer little resistance. Still, any resistance at all meant that the Federals were waking to danger; whatever the Army of the Valley was going to do must be done quickly.

Friday morning the army stirred early in the camps. Marching orders put Ramseur on the road from Sharpsburg to Boonsboro; Breckinridge's corps moved out of Rohrersville and took the highway for Fox's Gap and Middletown with Gordon in the lead. Rodes' men marched from the vicinity of Rohrersville southeast through Crampton's Gap in South Mountain.[20] Even the hardened marchers of the Army of the Valley felt the strain during the day. Upward they toiled, dust rose in clouds, and when a halt was called in the afternoon, the men were road weary and begrimed. They fell into bivouac gladly, Breckinridge's and Ramseur's men near Middletown and Rodes' near Jefferson.

Early established headquarters on the western foot of Catoctin Mountain.[21] The valley, the mountain, all the surrounding country was familiar to him and to many in the ranks. Gordon took time during the day's march to show some of the new staff the position on South Mountain where two years before D. H. Hill had grimly held the crest while Lee's scattered columns concentrated to battle McClellan. Early, whose interest in old glories never flagged, doubtless looked at the former battlesites with interest, but he could waste little daylight in recollection. Headquarters had been strategically located: from the foothills of Catoctin, the commanding general could keep in touch with Ransom's troopers, still holding the Pass to Frederick, and could plot the routes to be followed on the morrow. During the evening of the eighth he came to grips with the puzzle presented by General Lee. Exactly what his role should be in the attempt to free the Point Lookout prisoners still eluded him, but he received the clear impression that he should avoid bringing attention to it by any special efforts. Still, he must have some cavalry in position to aid if the need arose. What force should do this duty, and who should command it? Hazardous duty it might be, for the detachment must go toward Baltimore, diverging far to the left of Early's intended line of advance. The force would have to be sufficient to maintain itself in hostile country, but not so large as to reduce fatally the limited efficiency of the army's cavalry. The commander would have to be a man of enterprise, and preferably someone who knew intimately the country from Frederick to Baltimore.

A courier found Bradley Johnson atop Catoctin. He had watched bitterly as the day passed and Ransom refused to let him descend from his perch and take his old home town. On the mountaintop the weather had been grim, rain spat intermittently, the troopers huddled in makeshift shelters, and cursed the evils conjured by the brass. Johnson shared the resentment of the men, but the courier's summons jolted him from his sodden rancor. Report at once to Army Headquarters! Down the western slope Johnson rode, found the road toward Middletown, and soon located Early's camp.

A touch of the cap, returned greeting, and Johnson found himself in serious conference. Early's solemn mein gained Johnson's full attention, and he listened carefully as Jubal outlined a mission that must be to any trooper's taste. Early explained that Johnson must take 800 men north of Frederick early the next morning. On the flank of the Army of the Valley, he would have to be vigilant and guard the left in the action

Early expected near the town. If all seemed to be going well for the Confederates, Johnson must then strike across Maryland, cut railroads and telegraph lines north of Baltimore, circle around the city, cut the B&O between it and Washington, and be at Point Lookout on the night of July 12. Some effort would be made to free the prisoners at the Point. The details were vague to Early, but he speculated that Johnson would probably have to take the freed Rebels in charge and march them to Washington where the army should be waiting. The ex-prisoners could then be armed from the large arsenals in the Yankee capital and join in further operations. Could Johnson do the job?

Jolted by the magnitude of the task, impressed by the responsibility, Johnson pondered briefly. He knew the country well, all the roads and byways. The march, he said, was more than could be accomplished in his allotted time; he had to cover almost 300 miles in less than ninety-six hours. And the prescribed four days did not take into account time lost burning bridges and wrecking track. Did Johnson think he might almost make it? Again, he could not promise; but he would do everything humanly possible to be somewhere within supporting distance at Point Lookout by the twelfth.[22] If his column was not at hand, it would not be for want of effort. Good. Move at early dawn.

The campsites selected for the army on the night of the eighth worked greater effect on the enemy than Early knew. Breckinridge's position near Jefferson seemed to threaten the town of Urbana, east of Catoctin Mountain, and well to the left and beyond Frederick—beyond Monocacy, for that matter. And if the Rebels reached Urbana, they would have a grip on the main artery into Washington from the northwest. Wallace knew he had to prevent this, and sent the overworked Eighth Illinois riding left to guard the flank. During the night of the eighth, the Federals fell back from Frederick and Wallace directed his force to hold the crossings of the Monocacy. By then he knew certainly that General James B. Ricketts' Division of the U.S. VI Corps was well on the way to the Junction; when it arrived he calculated he would have about five or six thousand men deployed along the river. How many Early was bringing against him—he knew Early commanded—Wallace could not say, and this was one consideration which made him decide to make a stand on July 9: to develop fully the strength of the enemy force and to establish beyond doubt the Rebel objective. Whatever the answers, a stand on the Monocacy River might buy precious time. By now he had told Halleck where he was and of the serious concentrations building beyond the mountains. Surely someone was urging help from Grant's army? In any event, Wallace had decided he would stand on a river next day—for Washington and perhaps for the Union. Though he could hardly stay Early's onslaught for long, he judged a brief moment on the Monocacy might mean a lifetime to the North.

It was a Saturday, and it dawned with balmy sky and bracing breeze. Its summer loveliness lulled some of Early's infantry into thoughts of faraway places and happy times. Beyond Catoctin the angry clatter of skirmish fire began almost with the dawn and made odd accompaniment to homesick musings.

Dismounted Rebel troopers, reinforced by Ramseur's veteran skirmishers, pushed Federal skirmish lines through Frederick by 8 A.M., and followed as the bluecoats turned southeastward toward the Monocacy River. While Ramseur's men fought the enemy rearguard, Early directed other troops to skirt Frederick and get on with the advance. Breckinridge's command circled south of Frederick, while Rodes prepared to support Ramseur's left flank when line of battle formed.[23]

Ramseur's lead elements soon reported stronger enemy

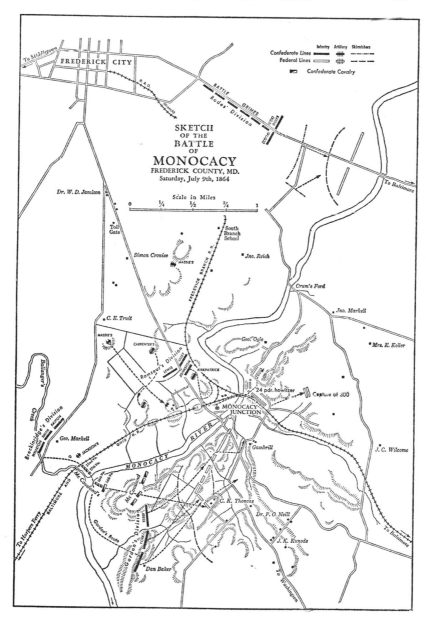

SKETCH
OF THE
BATTLE
OF
MONOCACY
FREDERICK COUNTY, MD.
Saturday, July 9th, 1864

Scale in Miles

resistance, the presence of infantry, and then a line of defense drawn beyond the Monocacy. Early, riding into Frederick, ordered his infantry to halt for deployment; he wanted to avoid blundering into a fight with his columns strung out on two roads and without accurate knowledge of Federal positions and strength. The infantry began to fan into battle formation about 9 A.M.

While this lengthy process took place, several Confederate guns opened up to smoke out Yankee cannon and almost immediately a heavy explosion pinpointed the location of a hostile 24-pounder howitzer, lesser explosions indicating field guns, but not in large numbers. Most of the cannon seemed to be north of the iron railroad bridge which carried B&O tracks over the river. South of the bridge, thousands of blue-coats were in line of battle.

While the artillery dueled away the morning and his men filed slowly into line, Early tended to business in Frederick. The town had the look of plenty; its coffers must be full, and surely the citizens would pay to save their lovely homes! He would spare the town, Early told the city authorities, if they contributed $200,000 to the Confederate cause. Mayor William G. Cole demurred: the sum could not be raised by a town boasting scarcely 8,000 people, and with liquid and intangible assets of not over $2,200,000. True, the large supply depot in the city made the place a legitimate military objective, and some payment would be made, but not $200,000! That or conflagration, said Jubal. The mayor and henchmen asked for time to debate methods of raising the money, and this Early could not refuse. He detailed William Allen, Wells Hawks and John Harman to wait in Frederick and prod payment while he went to the front.[24]

First glance at the Federal positions convinced Early that July 9, 1864, might well be a long, long day. As he rode out

of the southeastern limits of Frederick, Jubal found himself
on a vast plain which stretched possibly two and a half miles
eastward to the Monocacy. Beyond the river lay green corn-
fields, open ground for a small distance, and then a range of
hills which screened Baltimore and partially screened Washington. Two main roads, Early saw, diverged in an opening angle
from the river, the Washington pike running to the right, the
Baltimore pike to the left. The B&O tracks shimmered brightly
eastward along the Washington road. Lew Wallace, no mean
foe, had selected his ground shrewdly, and established a two-
mile front which covered all three avenues to the east. On the
Confederate left a Yankee force guarded a stone bridge over
the river and also the Baltimore road. The Union center was
anchored at the iron railroad bridge and guarded an old
covered bridge a little distance south of the railroad. The
wooden span took the macadamized Washington pike across
the Monocacy. Wallace's center was strengthened by a stern-
looking blockhouse. A sweep of his glasses toward the right
showed Early that the flank approaches to the Washington
highways were held by a large force of enemy infantry arrayed
in line of battle. There were more Yankees there than Frederick citizens had reported; apparently the "100-day militia"
men—which Early knew had been called up—were there in
large numbers. At least 7,000 Yankees barred the path of the
Army of the Valley.[25]

Sharp firing on the left indicated that Robert Rodes had
quickly deployed, shaken out a curtain of skirmishers, and
was attacking the bluecoated line on the western end of the
stone bridge. In the center Early heard the heavy boom of
the 24-pounder, and the lighter reports of smaller field pieces.
Ramseur's skirmishers were threading their way through wheat
fields and were working into the acute angle made by the
main line of the B&O and the Frederick spur. Soon Ramseur

would be in position to attack the iron and covered bridges.[26]

The fighting had not yet reached battle proportions; it was a combat restricted to skirmisher and artillery probing, each side trying to make the other develop full strength. And while time remained, Early determined to make a careful study of the field.

Like his old mentor, Stonewall Jackson, Early had trouble understanding the lay of land. Strategic import of geography came slowly to him and he knew it. Not many weeks before he had bungled part of his battle at Payne's Farm because he rushed into action without taking time to get his bearings. This time he would be cautious, survey the front carefully. He knew as soon as he saw the strength of the Federal position that a frontal assault would kill more men than he could afford. A turning movement seemed the only alternative. Clearly Wallace had most of his men already in position; he could not extend his front much further; consequently, a flank attack might roll up his whole line.

Early did not have to debate which flank to attack. His objective was the Yankee capital, and he needed to get control of the Washington pike as quickly as possible. If Wallace's left were smashed, the road would be open to the Rebels. Early, then, would send columns to his own right. But where could his men best cross the Monocacy? It was no mean barrier in itself, and a ford must be found. Jubal rode along the front, tobacco plug working furiously. Surely there was a ford somewhere!

By 11 A.M. the sun beat down on the field with oppressive force. Early noticed it, and it worried him for a special reason: increased temperature marked the passage of time. He could ill afford to burn too much daylight here; every minute counted if he were to reach Washington before Grant's veterans arrived. The ford had to be found, and quickly. But it had to be a

good one, one which offered access to the other side of the
river at some relatively unexposed point.

Anxiously Early rode and looked. Suddenly, a line of gray
cavalry cantered into view on the right, splashed across the
Monocacy about a mile below the wooden bridge and dismounted in line of battle. Furiously and steadily the troopers
attacked the Federal left, drove it back and captured a Federal
battery. McCausland's command it was, coming in from an
expedition against railroad and telegraph communications
between Harpers Ferry and Washington!

McCausland, as usual, had made an error. There were too
many bluecoated infantry in front of him; he could not hold
his ground, and would be thrown back. But impetuosity could
be forgiven him this time. He had found a ford for Early.

Instantly Jubal took advantage of the chance. Back to
Breckinridge's corps, held in reserve on the road to Frederick,
he sent a courier with urgent orders: advance to the front,
cross at McCausland's ford, deploy and support the cavalry
assault.

Breckinridge's men had been watching the slowly building
battle. In the uncommon role of spectators, they had been
kibitzing with gusto, cheering Rebel advances, jeering reverses.
Sitting in the road, in neighboring fields, anywhere they could
get a good view, the men had erected shelter tents against the
sun and were enjoying the sport. Most of them saw the lone
rider galloping furiously up the road, a billowing cloud of
dust fanning out behind him. Straight to General John Gordon
he rode, saluted, and presented a dispatch. Gordon read it,
spoke to some nearby officers, and mounted. Along the lines
of spectators rang the order: "Take arms!—no time now for
blankets, but get in your places at once! Right face. Forward
march!" [27]

No more unpopular order could have been given Gordon's

lazing veterans. Just when they were beginning to enjoy the day, they were told to leave behind the few possessions they had managed to save and get into the fight. They minded not so much getting into the fight as leaving behind blankets, oilcloths, little luxuries. This was most inconsiderate of the brass, the result, obviously, of bad planning!

Gordon paid no heed to the angry grumbling; he rode toward the right to inspect the ford, and when his men came up he ordered them to cross quickly and file left toward the blue line of battle.[28]

With the steadiness of veterans under artillery and skirmish fire, Gordon's men filed along a small path and splashed into the river. Happily the steep bank on the Yankee side hid them from view when they reached the water, and the actual crossing proved easy enough. But the same banks which offered a haven when crossing became a trap once the men were on the other side. Steep they were, muddy, and the Confederates slipped and slithered toward the top. When they came to the brow of the bluff a volley greeted them from a commanding ridge and Gordon's vanguard flinched, gathered themselves and rushed out on the field, rifles at the ready and automatically fanning into line of battle. Gordon, who had galloped across the Monocacy ahead of his men, observed that his column came swiftly and that his brigades formed rapidly in echelon from the right. He planned to attack heavily the enemy left elements and gradually extend pressure along the whole line so that the flank could get no help. Even though the men came as fast as possible, deployment took so long! While regiments and brigades formed front, the pace of battle seemed suddenly to slow down. Events stretched out and minutes lingered like hours.

On the Federal hills overlooking the river, however, time shortened, minutes were instants; fleeting impressions were all

the Federals gleaned of the Rebel crossing. From a command
post near the Union front, a tall, big-framed officer, Jim Ricketts, gazed along the Rebel positions with his glasses.[29]

When first he had been ordered by Grant to take his division
to Baltimore, he understood some sort of threat loomed against
Washington. And when he arrived at Baltimore on July 7,
chaos and incipient disorganization convinced him the threat
appeared real enough to the local citizenry. What he had been
able to learn from Baltimore army officers and from a dazed
War Department indicated that the high command understood
that Rebels were coming, but where they were, where they were
going, or what they intended no one knew. Only from Monocacy had come a semblance of sense; General Wallace had called
for help, and this indicated that somewhere in the welter of confusion somebody had taken action.

Part of Ricketts' Third Division—one of three divisions of
the U.S. VI Corps—moved from Baltimore expectantly, but
not even Ricketts foresaw the situation which existed at
Monocacy. The sad faced Wallace had stunned him when he
announced that Jubal Early lurked beyond the Maryland
mountains. Ricketts thought Early still held a segment of Lee's
front near Petersburg. Next, the Indiana general had surprised
him with word that he had only 2,500 men and with these
was determined to make a stand on the river. Now that Ricketts' division had arrived, Wallace admitted he felt stronger.

Ricketts agreed immediately with Wallace's estimate of the
strategic situation: a stand at the Monocacy had to be made,
else all the routes eastward would be offered to the enemy.
But he could not agree about the strength of their tactical
situation. An attenuated line of at least two miles, scarcely
a full field battery, only one heavy gun, the front cut by main
roads and by at least one important stream, exposed and vulnerable flanks—this picture hardly filled Ricketts with enthusi-

asm. He thought Wallace's guess that Early would attempt to turn the left was correct, and took the post of heavy responsibility on that flank. The morning burned on, and he watched with professional approval as Rebel columns curled along the roads, as gray skirmishers paced forward with precision, as batteries unlimbered smoothly for action. The popping fire which eddied along the river bank gave him notice the enemy was coming, and as the threat built to attack proportions around midday, he informed Wallace that Rebel units were crossing the river almost half a mile beyond his line and he would need help.

Wallace could see that, but there were no reserves to send —every man held a place in line. The only thing to do, Wallace did. Orders went swiftly to the men holding a *tête-de-pont* at the far end of the covered bridge: fire the bridge and covering blockhouse and fall back to the eastern shore. These men would provide a small addition to Ricketts' lines. Soon smoke drifted from the bridge, licking flames spread along the ancient timbers, and the old gray structure was lost in char and ash.

Still the Rebels poured over the river, kept drifting to Ricketts' left and extending the front. At about 1:30 P.M., a long line of gray figures burst from a blur of woods about 700 yards in Ricketts' left front. Several brigades there were, with clouds of skirmishers ahead, banners waving, guidons flapping, swords flashing in the sun. If they came on as they started, the Rebs would strike the Federal flank, overlap it, and roll up Ricketts' line toward the river. Now Ricketts did what he had feared for some time he must do. An order went to all his embattled troops: give up present positions, fall back and change fronts; put the right of the division on the river bank, and bend to the left to run roughly parallel with the Washington pike and cover it as far as thin ranks would allow. Dangerous under the most favorable circumstances, this

maneuver was hazardous in the extreme under fire. But the VI
Corps had been in tighter spots. Rapidly and in excellent
order the men shifted, formed new lines and re-emplaced their
field guns.[30]

The change in front did not escape John Gordon's notice.
That it had been well executed must have given him a moment's
pause; hardly could "100-day men" perform such a maneuver
so well under such a storm of shell and musketry. Those men
must be seasoned soldiers. But whoever they were, they must
be routed.

Gordon's initial attack on the enemy flank had been made
by Brigadier General Clement Evans' brigade on the far
right and Evans had fallen, badly wounded, in the advance.
On Evans' left, two demibrigades under Brigadier General Zeb
York had attacked and were shaken up somewhat. Still more
to the left, and in reserve, Gordon held Terry's men. Their
chance was almost at hand.

In front of Gordon's division loomed not only long lines of
blue infantry, but also unexpected hazards of terrain. The
fields that separated the Union and Confederate lines were
thickly dotted with grain-stacks—broad and high enough to
constitute a real barrier. So, too, the farm fences which marked
the fields. Troops moving toward the enemy lines would have
to thread through the grain and demolish fences under fire.
But the action was on, and Gordon knew he had to press it.
At about 2:30 P.M., while the Federals still were settling in
new positions, Gordon threw York's Louisianians at them and
drove the Union first line pell-mell into a second. A brief halt
to let his men catch breath and regain a semblance of
organization, then forward again. The roar of close musket
fire rose fierce and shrill, shellbursts added to the din, and
then over all the noise filtered the eerie, quavering Rebel Yell.
The second Federal line rocked back across a stream—which
Gordon noted ran red with blood—and broke for the rear.[31]

And just as a complete rout of the Federals seemed within his grasp, Gordon saw it—and a third blue line, longer than his, stretching left and right. If he struck it front on, he would be overlapped from both directions, and already a withering fire cut into his left elements. Halt the attack, regroup. While his men reorganized, Gordon pondered.

The Confederates apparently were outnumbered on the immediate field, but a fresh brigade hurled at the right spot might break that third Union line, drive it over the Washington pike and clear the way for Ramseur to cross the river and join the fray. Here was the spot for Terry. Orders went to him: attack toward the left, smash the Yankees who were delivering the searing flank fire.

Left oblique! Forward! and Terry's men began their attack. Out in front stood a field of waist-high corn, and beyond the field a post and rail fence. Behind the fence splashes of fire and smoke identified the Federal front. Into the field the skirmishers dashed, the whole brigade on their heels. Instantly Federal rifles shifted from flank to point-blank fire, and gray-clads began to fall. Still onward through the cornfield, closer to the line of smoke, now the men were running, all thought of organized lines gone. The screeching yell again rose, the men hurled themselves at the fence, and the Yankees broke and ran back.

But limited success was not enough. Gordon saw he needed more men to stabilize his line and dispatched two staff officers with a request for another brigade. Word came soon that help would arrive, but much time would elapse before it reached Gordon. He could ill afford to wait. If he lost the initiative of attack, he might lose what had been gained at heavy cost. The advance must continue with the men he had. Terry must change front, move left and assail the Federal right while the rest of the division stormed the front.

Huddling behind their hard-won fence, Terry's men gasped

for breath and made ready to storm to the next fence. But while they rested an officer rode up and down the line, shouting that they were in the wrong place. On another part of the field General Gordon waited for them. They must hurry back through the cornfield, circle along the lee edge of a hill, and march to the general. As soon as the word spread, men began running back, singly, in pairs, in groups, and quickly the field cleared of gray uniforms.

When the brigade had re-formed, Terry marched it to the left, farther upriver, and finally turned toward the top of a hill. Up there, quietly sitting on his horse, was John Brown Gordon. Alone he was, serene and calm. But the sleeves of his red shirt were hitched a little high, and that told the veterans all they needed to know: Gordon's fighting blood was up. As the head of the column toiled toward the pinnacle, Gordon reined around, dug spurs, and galloped to meet them. "Hurry up, boys," he said, turned his horse again and led the brigade toward a fence. Some of the men near the van caught sight of a second fence about two hundred yards ahead and of a line of Federal infantry marching along it toward the river. The enemy marched at the double quick, arms in right-shoulder shift, and looked to one Rebel as though they were on dress parade.

The sight of the Federals was too much for Confederate composure. From the Rebel vanguard came a yell, "At them, boys!" and the brigade prepared to rush headlong into the enemy column. Gordon, wisely riding at the point, whirled in his saddle and called "Keep quiet, we'll have our time presently. Some of you pull down the fence, so that we may go through!"

Many hands tore at the rails, a gap opened, the men stepped back and let Gordon ride ahead. He tried to keep excitement down, to steady the men, but he could feel the tension building.

Briefly he held check on the brigade, but after about 100 men had pushed through the gap in the fence, enthusiasm triumphed over discipline. "Charge them! Charge them!" the men screamed. Nothing could have held them back, one of them later recalled, "nothing but a shot through each man." The bunched leaders of the column ran ahead and reached the fence ahead of the Yankees. Quickly now, Confederates fanned out along the fence, aimed and fired. The first volley smashed into the flanks of the surprised Federals, stunned them, broke them. Back they ran. More and more of Gordon's men reached the fence and fired into the fleeing blue mass.

Aligned again, and with some semblance of discipline, Terry's men spilled over the fence. There was an indescribable battle excitement among them as they ran forward. The Rebel Yell floated over the whole battlefield, was echoed on the western bank of the river and re-echoed far upriver at the stone bridge. So chilling did it come that Wallace noted it and would later recall it as a "vent to battle passion strangely unlike that of any other of the great fighting Anglo-Saxon families."

Down the sloping hill ran the gray infantry, firing sporadically, but mostly just running to catch the foes. The line looked ragged, wavy, but it held together; puffs of smoke bobbed above it here and there, the whitish-blue burst of an enemy shell sprang in front now and then, and always the huddle of bluecoats tumbled ahead. Now the attack picked up all along the line; the Louisianians to the right charged, smashed through fences. And suddenly the whole Union front collapsed.

Ricketts urged his men back across the Washington pike and on toward the Baltimore road which had been designated as the avenue of retreat. Soon the Federals abandoned the railroad bridge and so opened the crossing for Ramseur's men. Now his division joined with Gordon, and shoved the Yankees

faster toward the rear. Incipient panic spread through the blue
ranks, and it was only by careful and brave management that
Wallace and Ricketts prevented an absolute rout. Even so,
the retreat disintegrated and finally became a thing of bits
and pieces. Occasionally a rear-guard line formed to sting
the pursuers, but Wallace's force ceased organized resistance.
By 4 P.M.[32] the day was over, the battle won for the Confederates. An old Rebel later recalled that it "was the most
exciting time I witnessed during the war." [33] The victors were
shaken, too, and were hardly in shape to pursue the battered
enemy. But Early cared little about pursuit. It was enough that
the Washington road had been cleared. More prisoners would
only retard the progress of the Army of the Valley anyway.

As sunlight turned orange over the scene of battle, the
commanding general checked on his situation. The army
seemed in fair shape; casualties did not exceed 700. Back in
Frederick, word of Confederate victory at last prodded the
reluctant city officials to find the cash for the $200,000 levy.[34]
Jubal's emissaries pocketed the contribution, gorged themselves on ice cream—rarest of delicacies—and rejoined headquarters. Everyone had had quite a day. Adjutant General
Sandie Pendleton, roaming the field with the General's orders,
had been the one who took word into Frederick in time to
close the financial negotiations. Kyd Douglas, stuck with
duty as Provost Marshal of the town, contrived to elude the
job during the latter part of the fight and took charge of
Ramseur's skirmish line just when Gordon's boys cleared the
way for them to cross the river and join the final assault. Glory
in good measure there was for all, and high praise for many.
Breckinridge, who watched Gordon's attack with pride, warmly
greeted the long-faced Georgian after the battle and remarked:
"Gordon, if you had never made a fight before, this ought to
immortalize you." [35]

Early moved headquarters across the river near the railroad bridge as firing died away to the east, and pondered some problems raised by the battle. Stiff resistance, reports from wounded Federals and from prisoner interrogation, confirmed the fact that part of Ricketts' Third Division, VI U.S. Army Corps, had been in support of Wallace's scratch command. This was important intelligence, and should have made Early proud, indeed. His expedition had caused sufficient alarm in high Union councils to provoke a detachment from Grant's army; and if rumor were correct, the rest of the VI Corps had also embarked for Washington. General Lee's diversion was beginning to work—at least to some extent. One objective had been achieved. But another objective had still to be considered. Now that he had definite knowledge of enemy reinforcements from the South, should Early proceed with his plan to attack Washington? Jube knew of the heavy fortifications which guarded all approaches to the Yankee capital; knew, too, that he could grasp the tempting prize only if there were few defenders in the forts. If numbers of bluecoats came up from Grant, the Confederates might be bloodily repulsed. Time remained the all-important factor. If Grant had sent only one division, Early could handle the situation, and if he had dispatched other troops tardily, Early might get to Washington soon enough to capture it. If, however, heavy reinforcements had reached the capital and the grayclads attacked recklessly, they might be obliterated, the entire army lost. Another consideration was Hunter coming on from the West. The Confederates could not delay long near Washington, else they surely would be caught from behind.

At the moment Jubal knew he could still escape south of the Potomac, but he never seriously considered the possibility. Audacity had proved its own reward, and Early's natural aggressiveness made it easy for him to see that opportunity justi-

fied risk. There could be no denying, however, that Wallace
had dealt a serious blow to the Confederate timetable. It was
now too late in the afternoon of July 9 to resume the advance,
and even had it been earlier, the army was tired and needed
rest from combat. At any rate, he would move forward on the
morrow.

The decision was the one which Wallace knew Early would
make, and it made the long, desperate hours on the river worth-
while. Wallace had deposited a day to the safety of the capital,
and had made Early develop his full strength. At last Grant and
Halleck had definite word about the Rebel expedition: Early
intended Washington as his objective, and he marched with
18,000, possibly 20,000 men. He had at least sixteen pieces of
artillery, probably more. And if the defenses of the capital were
unmanned, something urgent best be done. Wallace's army had
done its best, and he regretted not one moment nor any of the
2,000 casualties.[36] The Rebs had lost vital time, and Wallace
had gleaned the information he wanted. In his highly drama-
tized *Memoirs,* Wallace would look back on the battle as one
of the most satisfying achievements of an unusually active life.
From the Monocacy battleground, he took his men back along
the Baltimore road, and left the Army of the Valley to other
hands.

Sandie Pendleton first got the word on what next Jubal
planned. Bring the wagons and trains over the river during the
evening, he was told, so that the army could start at early dawn.
Send a messenger to learn how Bradley Johnson fared, and inform Breckinridge that his corps would take the lead as the
march began the next morning; he must point the column
southeastward on the road toward Rockville. Rodes would be
in the center, Ramseur the rear guard. Speed should be enjoined, the men urged to as fast a pace as their tired feet would
permit.

If the day of the battle had been hot, Sunday was hotter. The infantry was seared, dust choked, for mile after mile and the day baked on without end. Early noted that straggling grew worse in the afternoon, but he could hardly blame his men. Through Urbana, Hyattstown, Clarksburg, the gray columns passed, and, when Breckinridge called a halt in the late afternoon, the army had covered no less than twenty miles—about half the distance to Washington.

Disturbing reports came from Ramseur during the day. A body of enemy cavalry followed the Confederate rear guard, hitting the line when possible, picking up stragglers, and harassing so sternly that Ramseur had been forced to halt and deploy several times. This delayed the rear elements and not all of the army reached bivouac until 1 A.M. of the eleventh.[37]

Early established headquarters near Gaithersburg, Maryland, about four miles from Rockville,[38] and reviewed the day's activity. Bradley Johnson had started for Baltimore, as per orders.[39] McCausland had been ahead of Breckinridge all day, skirmishing with assorted Federal cavalry outfits, and about 3:30 P.M. fought a brisk engagement with outposts of the Second Massachusetts Cavalry, under Major William H. Fry.[40] Briefly stopped, McCausland, who learned every day, finally attacked the enemy and drove them beyond Rockville. Apparently all the Federals had between Washington and the Army of the Valley was cavalry. If true, the greatest prize of all lay less than a day's march away—Early's for the taking.

The Sabbath's fiery sun set at last. For Washington the red light in the west had special portent.

5

---- * ----

LET US BE VIGILANT,
BUT KEEP COOL

—A. LINCOLN

WAR RAGED all around Washington, and, although its position gave it a special vulnerability, the city stood curiously aloof. Thrust into Virginia like the spearhead of Union, the capital of the United States had been an immediate objective of the Rebels. They had come close—at First and Second Bull Run, at Antietam, even at Gettysburg—and, like Richmond, Washington had felt the terror of alarm and rumor. But war had not crashed at the gates; the sound of enemy cannon had been heard, but not at the threshold. Not since Dolly Madison hastily departed the White House and the British had touched torches to the city had Washington been under attack.

And by the summer of 1864 Washingtonians had developed a certain justifiable confidence. After all, the war raged now at the enemy's door; Richmond lay under siege and thousands of boys in blue were poised along twenty miles of trenches near Petersburg, almost ready to deliver the assault which would carry the Rebel capital. The alarms of 1862 and 1863 were all but forgotten; the "enemy" seemed a shadowy menace dim in the distance.

But Washington had fought its own special war. Through three hard years Washington denizens had watched and listened as Abraham Lincoln and a captious Congress wrangled, fought, patched, and legislated a war effort. They watched as the men called out by Congress tramped the dusty streets on the way south. They dug into their pockets for a little more as the national taxes soared. They paid dear for scarce food and commodities. And the old hands looked in wonderment at the thousands of newcomers who swelled the Federal payroll and clustered in the burgeoning bureaucratic offices and busy shops. Washington became the headquarters of the war; from it went the orders and the supplies and the men to fight in Virginia and on obscure fields in distant states. And because it was the heart of the Union, it had a special place in the plans of the warmakers.

President Lincoln, Congress, even some Union generals, recognized that to lose Washington would be to lose more than a city—to lose Washington might be to lose the war. Not certainly, but possibly. And it was a possibility that had shaped military policy since the beginning of the war; defense of the capital had become firmly fixed in Federal command decisions. To ensure the sanctity of the City, Union engineers had encased it in thirty-seven miles of heavy earthworks buttressed with palisades, forts, and heavy cannon. So formidable were the defenses that Washingtonians had long since ceased to think of them.[1] Behind the ramparts the capital endured its own conflict of nerves and politics.

To any who bothered to think, Washington's parallel with Richmond must have been disconcerting. Richmond, the heart of the Confederacy's tottering war effort, always had been the main objective of the Union. While Federal armies in remote areas combated with Rebel armies of dim renown, the Army of the Potomac—almost Washington's own—had struggled against the dust, the mud, the snow of North Virginia, and the thin gray lines of Robert Lee in apparently endless campaigns toward Richmond. Time and again the army had advanced from Washington, only to come back beaten. Yet Federal dedication to capturing the political symbol of Rebeldom remained constant. Might not the Rebels cherish a similar dedication?

Worriers along these lines were few or inarticulate. Behind the miles of earthworks, Washington's life went on. True, it had been vastly changed by the war: the gaiety of congressional seasons had faded somewhat; the lushness of levees had succumbed to a respect for national sacrifice. An easy, almost Southern business pace had vanished in a frenzy of activity, and the city's once spacious streets and malls teemed with the hordes of government workers. Housing was scarce, prices were high and graces lacking. This war was one of organization and logistics, requiring a huge corporate structure to run it. And Washington, like the United States generally, had become a business community with a new set of morals and a different philosophy of life.

Still it served as the great and charming symbol of the nation. All the old traditions of the Federal Union, all the ghostly memories of past heroes centered in its great halls, its offices, and hotels. But it was, too, a symbol of modern times: the center—as well as the generator—of power.

Part of the strength of the city came from its principal resident. Many presidents had made an impression on Washington, but none had been quite like Abraham Lincoln. The city had known him some years before the war, when as a roughhewn country lawyer, he represented an Illinois district in the House. But there had been little to distinguish him then; he made some speeches for the Wilmot Proviso, and had been a good Whig. Now he was President of the United States. When he came to occupy the White House, there were things about him to re-

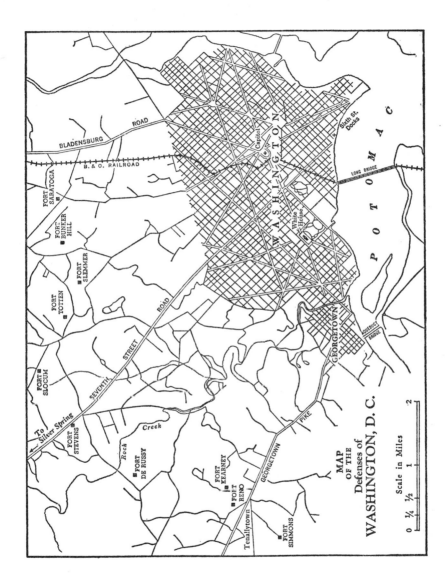

MAP
OF THE
Defenses of
WASHINGTON, D.C.

mind old Washingtonians of Andrew Jackson: back-country
manners, appeal to commonfolk, an earthy humor, long-limbed
awkwardness, and ill-fitting clothes. In the terrible crisis of se-
cession he spoke in parables and non-sequiturs, joked in times
of solemn portent, and showed a shocking paucity of tact. The
best hope appeared to be in some members of his cabinet, but
even with sound men like Seward and Welles, and later Stanton, it seemed the country had doomed itself to incompetence
at the time of sternest testing.

Old residents made up their minds about public servants
slowly. Long experience made cynics of many, but even cynics
delayed final assessment of Lincoln until he should blunder ir-
retrievably. He didn't. The test of Sumter he passed with acu-
men; he issued his volunteer call with direct honesty, and
managed the growing war effort with developing finesse. From
the White House and the War Department, he watched the
course of the war. Through the gruelling defeats of 1861, 1862,
and 1863, he stood firm. The country came to count on him;
in defeat he encouraged, in victory he praised and cautioned.
The city knew him now as no ordinary man. Iron and velvet,
he was. The Union must be saved, and he would stick to the
objective until the end. But he cried for all the thousands who
sprawled on Southern fields, and he transcended causes to
grieve for both sides. He loomed as a figure of almost pre-
ternatural grandeur. His craggy face showed the ravages of
suffering, his eyes spoke the compassion of a great heart.

Time and circumstance enhanced his native shrewdness. By
1864 his political foes, and there were many, conceded his
damnable cleverness; his friends, and there were some, knew
his wit, his charm, his dauntless determination. He had become
a deft politician, a sound war leader. He knew how to use op-
ponents wisely, to cherish friends, and to bend when the crisis
of his cause demanded. With the growth of political wisdom

came greater depth of insight. His natural humor and long-standing interest in people gave him a perspective and sympathy rare in public men. The crucible of war added some ineffable ingredient to his language and made him eloquent beyond his time. When he spoke on the war, on its horrors, on hopes for the future, his words echoed down to history with lasting compulsion. He was, by 1864, tempered by experience and tested by defeat. Even the careful Washingtonians gave him allegiance as an able chieftain.

Lincoln had assumed the role of war leader without much military experience, and that was all to the good. Across Mason and Dixon's Line, Jefferson Davis' troubles with his generals clearly showed the grief caused by a chief executive who commanded when he should have been planning. Lincoln's martial experience had been confined to a stint with militia in the Black Hawk War, where his derring-do as a gawking captain pleased him immensely. All he knew about war was that he scarcely excelled in the military art, and he had best rely on his generals. In most instances he would have been right, of course, but his generals—at the outset—were hardly ones to count on. They soon almost convinced him that the comical snarls of the Black Hawk campaign were not uncommon, that an innate idiocy lurked in all military matters.

But he reacted to the crisis of command as he did to political troubles. Since he had no professional militarism to ensnarl him in regulations, he experimented, groped toward a command system which would enable him to find a general to run the war while he organized the country to sustain the armies. First he called on General Winfield Scott, whose fame dated back to the War of 1812, to run the Union's effort, and next he called on the Little Napoleon, George B. McClellan. These two planned well, but Scott was just too old and too obese to take the field, and cautious McClellan would not go when he

General Jubal Anderson Early, C.S.A.

Union forces (foreground) repel a Confederate assault on a part of the line around Washington

President Lincoln visits the battleground at Fort Stevens

General John Brown Gordon, C.S.A.

Major General Lew Wallace,
U.S.A.

got there. Other generals Lincoln called to command, a dismal list of them: John Pope, Ambrose Edward Burnside, Joseph Hooker, William Starke Rosecrans, Don Carlos Buell, J. A. McClernand, John C. Fremont (the Lost Pathfinder), Judson Kilpatrick ("Kilcavalry" to the horse soldiers). When these all failed him during the terrible frustrations of the war, Lincoln had been forced to try his hand at command, but his orders were ill-executed by nincompoops, and he continued to look for a man to run the Federal armies. Henry Halleck, the stolid scholar, looked to be a likely prospect, but he soon lost himself in endless redtape.

The man Lincoln sought came from the western theater. He rose out of the ashes of broken hopes along the Mississippi, and he seemed about as unlikely a prospect for supreme command as could be found. U. S. Grant had come from a half-forgotten career in the Old Army and off a Missouri farm to lead U.S. troops in the west. He had his share of failures—a bad day at Shiloh, a wrecked campaign at Holly Springs—but he plugged along with Job-like patience and drab tenacity. The Vicksburg campaign earned him Lincoln's heartfelt praise, and called him to the President's attention as a potential supreme commander.

In March, 1864, Lincoln made his major command decision. Grant, called from the west, received the rank of Lieutenant General—the highest in the Federal army—and the title of General-in-Chief of the Armies of the United States. His assignment: win the war.

Grant had a plan. It lacked almost everything in subtlety and grace; it had no sparkle, no elegance, but it showed that he was the one general who understood clearly the nature of the war. Use the armies, was his plan, in building a huge crusher. Attack all along the Confederacy's embattled frontier, press every Rebel army to the limit, use the Union's vast superiority in men, money, and sinews of war. Grant, soon known as the

Hammerer, was a logistician, a military businessman, and he knew that the Confederacy could not long last in a stern war of attrition. This clear realization lay behind his relentless smashing in the Wilderness, behind the awesome butchery at Cold Harbor, the constant sliding by the left flank until finally twenty miles of trenches scarred the countryside south of Petersburg.[2] If the maneuvering in May and June had not beaten Lee, it had at least shoved him into a siege, and if this had not been all that Grant desired, it was the thing Lee could least afford. Sherman, carrying out a major part of Grant's 1864 strategy, hacked at Joe Johnston and the Rebel Army of Tennessee, pushed them back inexorably on Atlanta, and made impossible the diversion of any troops to Virginia. As long as manpower held out, and the will to fight sustained the Union, the campaign would proceed. It had begun around Washington, the city had seen the new legions march southward over the old well-traveled roads, and this time it looked like the men would bring victory when they came back. The city served as the main base for them, and this made the operations around Richmond especially poignant to the capital's citizens. They felt that the Army of the Potomac was their own, that each replacement who filed south was theirs.

Men were the big issue. By July, 1864, casualty lists filled column after column in northern newspapers; the cost of the Wilderness, Spotsylvania, Cold Harbor, Petersburg, Rocky Face Ridge, Dalton, the Etowah, Kenesaw Mountain, the Chattahoochie, was told in the endless, impersonal statistics. The Union shuddered at the price, but Lincoln asked for more men, and for a time, at least, he would receive them.

All day on the glorious Fourth, Washington waited for news everyone confidently expected. It was a day for big things, especially with Grant running the Army of the Potomac. Old Meade, in actual command of the army, was one who had wasted this day—fresh in mind was the awful July Fourth delay after Gettysburg a year earlier—but Grant had made that selfsame day his own when he had coldly informed John Pemberton that the terms for Vicksburg were unconditional surrender. Surely on this anniversary of his elevation to the Union's pantheon of heroes, he would break Lee's thin cordon of defense or make some other stellar stroke for victory. But the day passed with no stirring news. The War Department did get one item of disconcerting intelligence: Sigel had been defeated and panic was creeping through the Shenandoah. But this hardly ruffled the summer lethargy of Secretary Stanton's office. Over on Georgetown Heights, Halleck roused briefly from torpid fascination with military pomp and circumstance, but soon lapsed back into routine. Guards trooped in and out of his quarters, banners flapped from his flagpole, and buglers sounded martial calls. Halleck waged war to the full in bloodless pantomime.

Those few who had a moment's worry over word from the west forgot it in the activity of the afternoon. With proper patriotic oratory, the first session of the Thirty-eighth Congress adjourned. On the White House lawn, huge crowds of Washington's Negro citizens gathered to enjoy a special, long-planned Sunday-school picnic. Here the spirit of freedom could be fully felt. On the outside of the group, sitting dejectedly on curbstones, was a motley assembly of Southern Negroes, "contrabands," the ones so much of the shouting was about. But in the complicated hierarchy of the Negro world, they did not belong—they were inferiors and not of the Free. Those who were "in" showed it by gay and costly clothes, plush carriages, and affluence apparent. More than ever before, the Fourth of July had meaning for them. And they savored it most of the afternoon.

In another part of town that day, quite a different sort of

gathering occurred. The Peace Democrats assembled to consider the political situation. The summer of 1864 would witness a fierce and fateful presidential campaign, and there seemed every possibility—if the dead continued to pile up along Grant's ditches—that the Peace Democrats could swing the election and bring an end to carnage. At least the prospect loomed large enough to discuss. And with news that Salmon P. Chase, controversial Secretary of the Treasury, had handed in his resignation once too often and Lincoln had accepted it, it came clear that dissatisfaction about the Union's finances had reached the highest counsels. Lost treasure, taxes, inflation, nibbled at the national will, and the growing doubt about the country's credit did more damage. Here were signs of morale failure to gladden the hearts of the timid. And the Peace Democrats hoped, long and hard.

Washington's theaters made a special thing of the Fourth. The season had been a highly successful one which had boasted memorable performances by hardy tragedian Edwin Forrest and by noisy and athletic John Wilkes Booth. It was to close at Ford's new theater. This assured a comfortable mob at Tenth Street between E and F, and a flattering reception for Miss Susan Denin in Dumas' *Three Guardsmen*. "Erasmus," the *National Intelligencer's* arbiter of things thespian, announced that he, for one, was glad the season approached *finis*. It did no good to "force the season," but he would miss Ford's sterling offerings. There were improvements to be made—Ford should strengthen the orchestra, add to the stock company—but his staging rivaled all others, and his judgment of the public's taste was unerring.[3]

The less fastidious fanciers of gaslight could take heart, however, for Leonard Grover's theater, on Pennsylvania Avenue near Willard's Hotel, remained open, and offered diverting burlesque operas, witty comedians, and "hits upon the times."

A popular blackface comic, Harry Macon, was ready to take up where the Forrests and Booths left off; he, and "the charming vocalist, Miss Mollie Bogart," were to lighten the mood between agonized acts of *Beau Sickman: or the Bushwackers of the Potomac*.

The city had no dearth of parlors of diversion. Out in the Northern Liberties, and even in respectable residential neighborhoods near Pennsylvania Avenue, bawdy houses offered solace from the drab government life or the rigors of the field. For sporting gentlemen of less active natures, there were ample gaming establishments—some noisome and disreputable, others quiet and plush. And for men who relished an evening's companionship amid the fraternal click of billiard balls, there were many happy locales. One of the most impressive, and most sanctified by historical association, was in Willard's Dancing Hall, now part of the large establishment of the enterprising Willard brothers. Once a church, later a sort of lyceum, and the site of the ill-fated Peace Conference of 1861, the Hall, in 1864 offered special attractions to men of the cue.

Let one observer, whose account was written only from a sense of prim and proper duty, describe the delectably iniquitous interior:

As you entered the doors, near either wall of the room, in former times a stairway led you to a neat gallery set apart for the use of the choir. These stairways had been removed and between them had been erected a *"Bar!"* This was a busy place. In front of it, was a crowd of men, old, young and middle aged, all engaged in the same general occupation. Some were sucking whiskey out of tumblers, through straws; others were sipping it through silver strainers—others still, were drinking it without any machinery; and the clinking of glasses, obscene jests; incipient quarrels and horrible blasphemy, which met the ear at the same time, formed a strange and singular medley. Behind the bar were three men. One of them, and

much the more gentlemanly of the three, was a negro, who
appeared to be quietly gazing upon the scene before him, except when he was occasionally called into service by one of
the executive ministers of the institution. These latter were
two old men in a condition of semi deshabille—their heads
were master pieces of the barbers art. They were hatless, coat-
less, cravatless with shirt sleeves rolled up to their shoulders;
their collars limp and sweaty. They were answering the varied
calls of their customers for "whiskey straight," "brandy smash"
"rum toddy" "Tom & Jerry" &c &c &c. with much activity.
They must have had the inexhaustable vessel of the conjuror
for they appeared to pour all these different liquors from the
same bottle, only varying the flavor with mint, nutmeg &c. and
the amount of perspiration which dripped from their steaming
arms and faces into the mixtures they were preparing. . . .
But that painting was never executed, which could produce the
effect now seen in Willard's Hall. It was so dim and dark, that
the lower end could scarcely be distinguished from the en-
trance where I stood. A painter only with a lively imagination
could portray the scene. On either side of the passage through
the middle, were five billiard tables. Over each of them were
four gas burners, arranged in the form of a Grecian Cross,
shedding their lurid light through the smoky haze. From side
to side across the hall were several wires tensely drawn upon
which were strung a large number of white and black buttons,
used in some way in counting the game. Along the wall racks
were builded in which were kept the ashen sticks, called cues
which were used to knock about the ivory balls in playing the
game. Hung between these racks were several pictures. One,
professed to be a copy of a photograph of *Phelan* who is said
to be the "father" of billiards upon this continent. Next hung,
which I suppose to have been an apotheosis of the game. It
was a pink faced Goddess, clothed in a scant dress, apparently
made up from a second hand American flag, with a blue cap,
partially covering yellow curls; suspended in mid-air with arms
etc, spread over a billiard table, around which were standing
several amateurs of the game, cue in hand, with their faces
turned skyward. Farther along was a picture containing the

reputed portraits of several eminent professors of the game, distinguished principally by low foreheads and fat beefy faces. Midway on one side was a small imitation pulpit over which was painted in large capitals the word "Cashier" flanked on either side by a framed set of the rules of the game the price of which was most conspicuous. . . . The style of conversation was very uniform. It was loud and boistrous, plentifully garnished with oaths, interspersed with passionate altercation, sometimes breaking out into coarse raillery or attempts at obscene wit. . . . There is one section of the Hall to which I have not particularly referred. There is in one corner, a table of peculiar construction. It had no "pockets" and on that account was best adapted to games of chance. Standing where I did at the upper end of the Hall I could only see a dense circle of men surrounding this table and filling the seats in proximity to it. True the smoky haze was thicker in that quarter than elsewhere, and the conversation though less boistrous was more profane. . . .[4]

By 1864 Washington had become a symbol of Union, a citadel of strength, a palace of pleasure and the main military base for Federal operations in the east. Gone were the days of genteel cynicism, refined sophistication. Cynicism and sophistication now were hard and brassy and well earned. The city felt the alchemy of progress.

Over in the War Department a different progress had begun to create unease. A welter of confused reports filtered in from the vicinity of Harpers Ferry. After July 4, the telegraph to Harpers Ferry went dead, and suddenly all that happened beyond Frederick, Maryland, lay shrouded in mystery. Major General Augur, commanding the Department of Washington, decided in face of bafflement in the War Office to send Colonel Clendenin, and the Eighth Illinois Cavalry toward Harpers Ferry on a scouting expedition.[5] And since Sigel appeared to have cracked up under the strain of fighting at Martinsburg and Harpers Ferry, and Weber seemed uncertain, Augur sent another general out to the threatened area in case a command change was required. Brigadier General Albion P. Howe received command of the 170th Ohio National Guard, some units of dismounted troopers, a light battery and orders to get to Harpers Ferry.[6]

The need for accurate information about the Rebels was desperate. General Weber obviously had lost perspective—he reported that there were at least 10,000 to 20,000 grayclads pressing around him. Augur didn't believe it, and Stanton was skeptical. On the other hand, Pennsylvania's governor, Andrew G. Curtin, became alarmed at the prospect of another Gettysburg incursion and asked for Federal assistance and information. Stanton could not afford to slight Curtin. He put Major General Darius N. Couch, a trusted officer, at the governor's disposal, and wrote to assure the state executive that Pennsylvania would be protected. On July 4, he observed to Curtin that "this Department has no accurate information as to the rebel force, but General Grant reports that Early's force has returned to the army in front of him. There is nothing yet received showing the enemy to be more than a cavalry force with some artillery." To pacify the alarmed governor, the Secretary added that the President authorized calling out the 100-day militia. But at the same time he assured Curtin that General Hunter could be expected at any moment from the remote fastness of western Virginia, and he would hit the ranging Rebels from the rear. The only item of concern in this last assurance was the fact that no communication had been received from Hunter in some little time.[7]

By Tuesday morning, July 5, Henry Halleck bestirred himself. In a querulous dispatch to Grant he complained that no one in Washington knew much about anything, that nothing had been heard from Hunter, and the oncoming Confederates might number as many as 30,000 men. If, he observed, there were one half as many as rumored, Washington had not enough men to deal with them. He thought Grant might well spare some help to the capital.

For months Grant had worked to build up sufficient numbers for his summer drive against Lee. Men came in slowly; all kinds of side demands siphoned them off to the periphery of war. At length, through the President's hard efforts, a large enough Union army ringed Richmond. Grant strongly objected to parting with a single man. Detachment of strength away from Richmond could well delay the summer offensive. Loath as he was to stall Petersburg operations by yielding to diversionary pressure, Grant could not ignore the threat to Washington. He agreed, if absolutely necessary, to dispatch a corps to deal with what he firmly believed to be no more than a small raiding party.[8]

Things changed at the War Office from moment to moment, and by afternoon of the fifth Halleck was informing Grant that Hunter had at last inched his way into the threatened sector, and still later that day remarked grandly that "I think your operations should not be interferred with by sending troops here. If Washington and Baltimore should be so seriously threatened as to require your aid, I will inform you in time." Sigel got into the confusion by sending a comforting dispatch on the fifth that no Rebels were north of the Potomac at any point east of Maryland Heights.[9] But nothing that hapless "Flying Dutchman" reported seemed worth crediting, nor, for that matter, did the dispatches of Weber. Halleck had a pretty clear understanding of his immediate commanders in the field, and characterized them to Grant:

> The three principal officers on the line of the [rail] road are Sigel, [Julius] Stahel, and Max Weber. You can, therefore, judge what probability there is of a good defense if the enemy should attack the line in force.[10]

Grant judged immediately, and this judgment, plus growing
indications that Early's corps and Breckinridge's division were
near Harpers Ferry, made him increasingly uneasy. Someone
else, he thought, ought to command north of the Potomac
until Hunter could come into contact with the enemy. His
candidate was Darius Couch, and he followed the suggestion
with an acid evaluation of poor Sigel:

> All of General Sigel's operations from the beginning of the war
> have been so unsuccessful that I think it advisable to relieve
> him from all duty; at least until present troubles are over. I
> do not feel certain at any time that he will not, after abandon-
> ing stores, artillery, and trains, make a successful retreat to
> some safe place.[11]

Need for change had been fairly clear, even to Halleck, and
he determined to put the defense of the capital in the hands of
someone who at least could collect his thoughts, if not many
troops. Couch already had a job advising the skittish governor
of Pennsylvania, and Halleck asked his friend Quincy Gillmore, lately an enemy of Ben Butler's, to come to Washington
and get a grip on chaos. Stanton's personal choice seemed to be
Alex McCook, of the famed "Fighting McCooks" from Ohio.
In the command crisis Lincoln became interested. Stoutly he
stuck to the idea of letting Grant run the army—he wanted to
keep hands off. But Sigel's feeble efforts confirmed the President in a lingering doubt, and on July 7, he issued a Special
Order making General Albion Howe commander of the district
of Harpers Ferry. Sigel was shelved and directed to report to
Hunter for whatever disposition he wanted to make of him.
This was hardly a fair fate, since Hunter already was busily engaged in fixing the wreckage of his department squarely on
Sigel's slumping shoulders.[12]

Things were in even worse confusion than Stanton, Halleck,

or Grant imagined. Orders were going in all directions. Hunter, trying to find out where Early was, could not seem to get beyond Cumberland, Maryland. Reports had Rebels intruding in all parts of southern Maryland and as far as Chambersburg, Pennsylvania. In the incipient disorganization, Lincoln called on the Governors of New York, Pennsylvania, Massachusetts and Ohio for 100-day men, and all save Curtin came through in handsome style. Curtain haggled over whether the men should be mustered into state or Federal service and thoroughly irked Stanton.[13] Halleck, moved to a burst of vigorous albeit confused energy, called for help from everywhere, only to find that the Union had yielded up every man to Grant's slaughter pens at Petersburg or to Sherman's meat grinder in Georgia.

Here was a terrible dilemma. For the first time there was a real and urgent manpower shortage. Arms were not a problem now, there were uniforms and rations aplenty, but the men were all with Grant and Sherman. With a large enemy aggregation already on Union soil, the heart of the Union lay bare and vulnerable.

Salvation lay with Grant, and he knew it. From his army would have to come reinforcements to save the capital, and perchance prevent the freeing of a great number of Confederate prisoners at the large and important prisoner-of-war compound at Point Lookout, Maryland.[14] He started some men toward Washington on the sixth: Ricketts' division of the VI Corps, plus some dismounted troopers—a total of about 8,000. And as increasingly serious word arrived from Washington, Grant's composure cracked slightly. Finally he heard that Major General Lew Wallace, who had long been at Baltimore in charge of the Middle Department, had taken a small force out to meet Early and had lost the Battle of Monocacy. Now Grant knew that nothing save scattered disorganized militia, some 100-day men and hordes of hysterical citizens stood between Jube and his objective.

In Baltimore, news of Wallace's defeat brought terror to the streets; alarm bells rang and all during the night of the ninth and tenth people rushed hither and yon searching for arms. At six o'clock on the tenth, the tocsin rang again. By then some small semblance of determination had seeped through anarchy. Above the pealing of the bells the sounds of fife and drum could be heard, and motley groups of irregulars marched to the city's works. If no one else would help, Baltimore would save itself!

The City Guard—a creaking and antiquated unit—along with some of the newly mustered and absurdly trained Union League clubs, milled toward the expected front. By 10 A.M. some 10,000 "troops" were in the streets en route to assorted fortifications. Not everyone responded to the emergency: secesh elements counseled caution, predicted dire things for the city when the Rebels took it, and boasted of their importance for the first time since the silencing of the Maryland legislature by Lincoln in 1861. But the loyal hordes drowned the voices of treason and hoped for a chance to cram the words down Southern throats later.

By the afternoon of the tenth, news came that the enemy had turned toward Washington. If this word caused a small deflation of enthusiasm, an occasional pang of frustration, most of the people reacted happily—the bravery of the morning had been sufficient unto the emergency. If Washington suffered, too bad—but better Washington than Baltimore.[15]

Washington's reaction to word of Wallace's defeat equaled Baltimore's, perhaps excelled it. The War Department by now had faint glimmerings of the deadly seriousness behind Jubal Early's endeavors, and knew with certainty that the capital's available defenders could be counted on for scarcely more than gallant sacrifice. This suspicion had leaked out to the populace, and fear sparked the air. It increased as refugees straggled in with exaggerated stories of outrage and destruction. So many of them came that a fearful shortage of shelter and food developed almost at once, and the economics of disaster went into effect: prices skyrocketed and hoarding increased.

Few citizens could have taken much heart from the government's defensive measures. Along with the lost and frightened refugees, the streets were choked with herds of horses being led this way and that, without apparent direction. Hastily organized bodies of irregulars marching to and fro did not noticeably increase the confidence of the populace, and had the citizens known the real extent of military muddling, they would probably have fled the city.

Especially would they have been appalled to know the extent of disorganization and disaffection among the highest commanders. Stanton and Halleck, of course, worked at normal cross-purposes. Each a man of ego, each ran his domain without benefit of the other's counsel. Possibly that was a good thing; ignorance can hardly improve incompetence. But, nonetheless, in a time of such emergency they should have worked together. Gideon Welles, caustic Navy Secretary, observed that "Halleck is in a perfect maze, bewildered, without intelligent decision or self-reliance, and Stanton is wisely ignorant. I am inclined to believe, however, that at this time profound ignorance reigns at the War Department concerning the Rebel raid . . . that they absolutely know nothing of it—its numbers, where it is, or its destination.[16]

Stanton and Halleck each had his own handpicked general arrive to take charge of something and even Grant sent his own favorite, E. O. C. Ord. Suddenly there was such a plethora of generals that Halleck acidly rejected the offer of assistance from one unattached brigadier with a gauche attempt at humor:

Washington, D.C.,
July 11, 1864.

Brig. Gen. J. R. West,
Fifth Avenue Hotel, New York.

We have five times as many generals here as we want, but are greatly in need of privates. Anyone volunteering in that capacity will be thankfully received.

H. W. Halleck,
Major-General and Chief-of-Staff.[17]

Military preparations appeared to be at an all-time low. At Chris Augur's harassed headquarters, the dismal condition of Washington's defense had plagued the knowing for weeks. The general had the dubious honor to command the Department of Washington and the XXII Corps, and on paper he counted 31,000 men available in the department. But the figures were illusory; not more than 20,000 were within support distance of the capital, and more than half of these were fragmented into tiny garrisons, patrols, bridge guards. After all detachments and other deductions were made, Augur might be able to put about 9,500 men in the thirty-seven miles of entrenchments. Again, statistics told only a half-truth. Quality was not measured in numbers, and the quality of Washington's defenders left almost everything to be desired. Most of the good soldiers had marched south to bolster Grant's lines, and what remained for the capital were inexperienced trainees, Ohio militiamen, the Veteran Reserve Corps (semi-invalids), and the raw, virtually useless 100-day men from various states.

Augur had protested the dispatch of most trained artillerists to the Army of the Potomac; he had tried to retain in the Washington defenses all the men who had trained on the big guns, but the cost of the summer campaign in Virginia had run so high that every available soldier was pulled into the infantry. This looked to Augur like pound-foolishness, but vast casualties always palsied the War Department and triggered a great search for "shirkers" behind the lines. Most of the old hands at the guns were now in the lines at Petersburg, their places taken by militiamen who could hardly be expected to recognize a breech from a barrel. Augur wanted at least one regiment of heavy artillerists sent back to him, but Grant had haggled at the suggestion and delayed as long as possible.

In this manpower crisis Halleck's order to General Howe to take reinforcements to Harpers Ferry had done more damage than good: it had reduced by almost one-third the available infantry strength along the northern defense perimeter. And if Early came at Washington from the area of Monocacy, he would hit the northern works, presently held by two militia regiments strong enough to man the earthen forts, but too weak to man the connecting rifle pits. So badly did Augur need infantry that he had to try to hold some five miles of line, roughly from Fort De Russy to Bladensburg, with one militia regiment!

Such comical depletion of strength at last got through to Halleck. While he urged the District Veteran Reserves into the line, rounded up convalescents and stragglers for temporary duty, he persuaded Grant to order the remainder of the VI Corps to Washington and to agree that the XIX Corps, coming to the Army of the Potomac from New Orleans, and the ill-starred Red River Expedition could go straight to the capital. But time would elapse before these additional veterans could arrive, and meanwhile Early's hardy infantry marched against works manned by barely one-fifth enough infantry and by only one shift of gunners.[18]

With every emergency, of course, comes great opportunity— for someone. At this moment of terrifying anxiety for the Union, Montgomery C. Meigs, able Quartermaster General of

the United States Army, entered the lists. For three years he
had tended the army's stores, had made the blue-coated soldiers
the most oversupplied in military annals, had worked industrial
and management miracles. More than almost anyone else, he
was the "organizer of victory," the Carnot of the North. But
beneath the businessman's brisk mein beat a heart longing for
glory in the field. And at last war had come to him. In the huge
shops, warehouses, and other establishments of the Washington
depots there were thousands of civilian employees. Earlier, in
times of anxious expectation of Rebel raids, the male workers
of the quartermaster department had been organized into
military units, drilled and made ready for the day when they
would do duty for their depot and their country. But so long
had the day been delayed that the organizations had decayed,
drilling ceased, muster rolls were no longer kept, rifles were
rusted. Now, suddenly, the day had come. Meigs offered himself and his followers to Halleck as the minutemen of Washington.[19]

The first flush of enthusiasm got a chill from Augur, who felt
that the imminent arrival of lead elements of the VI Corps
would make the use of government employees unnecessary—
and surely that would be a double blessing. Some valuable
civilians could get killed in the works, thus reducing the effec-
tiveness of factories, and, in addition, the confusion of civilian
volunteers would further confound bedlam. But Meigs persisted. The VI Corps progressed up the Potomac with madden-
ing sloth—quarter-master troops might yet be needed, and he
intensified preparations for mobilizing.[20]

Halleck, for his part, was ready to use everybody. There
was talk of calling out the District of Columbia Militia—final
confession of bankruptcy! And in what must have been the
ultimate surrender, Halleck accepted with almost heartfelt
gratitude the offer of Welles to put in the lines some 1,000 em-

ployees of the Washington Navy Yard if the army needed help.[21] With these ragtag units, Halleck, Augur, Gillmore, Mc-Cook, Meigs, and finally Grant's friend Ord, would have to hold Washington through Sunday, July 10. Not until Monday could the rest of the VI Corps be expected, nor substantial numbers of the XIX Corps.

Two things stood clearly revealed by the scrambling for men on July 8 and 9—some coherent pattern of command would have to be worked out, and a survey must be made of the over-all condition of Washington's defenses. How many men were where, in what state of readiness, and with what equipment?

As for the command structure, it was amazingly compli-cated. Augur ostensibly commanded the whole show; the de-partment was his and what went on in it legitimately came under his charge. But Gillmore, McCook and Ord had wan-dered into the picture, and each was given charge of a segment of the lines or of some rear echelon establishment. Then there was the problem of Colonel Moses N. Wisewell, Military Gov-ernor of Washington, whose duties spilled over to the command of troops.[22] A spirit of wholehearted cooperation was notice-ably absent, and delicate questions of authority constantly arose. But command problems seemed small, indeed, com-pared with the urgent necessity for men and information.

Scarcity of cavalry kept the city still in ignorance about Rebel numbers, but all knew by now that the enemy came in considerable strength. If it seemed impossible to learn about the enemy, it appeared almost as difficult to find out anything concerning the condition of outlying district posts. "What about the Potomac defenses?" wondered Halleck and Augur. The bridges, at least, ought to be well covered, since attention had long focused on the possibility of a Rebel cavalry dash across the river and into Georgetown or Washington.

On July 6, however, Halleck received a sickening report

from Lieutenant Colonel B. S. Alexander, aide to General
J. G. Barnard, Chief Engineer of the Washington defenses.
Alexander had gone on an inspection tour of the Washington
bridge defenses and was horrified at what he found. The famous Chain Bridge, above Georgetown, was in charge of a
small detachment of Veteran Reserves, with the batteries on
the Washington shore under the separate command of a private who knew nothing about the guns, not even how to load
them! The lieutenant commanding the bridge detachment
thought the span was mined, but as Alexander observed, "he
must be mistaken as I have never heard that the piers . . .
are mined." Of the Acqueduct Bridge, on the road leading
from the edge of Georgetown to Falls Church, Alexander noted
that there were several blockhouses on the Virginia approaches,
but they were not manned. The main defense proved to be a
stockade with a huge gate on the Virginia shore. The Veteran
Reserve captain in charge stoutly maintained he would close
the gate and put his thirty men at the stockade walls the moment any hostile force approached, but he then confessed
lamely that he did not know if the gates would close, or if
there were any bars available to bar them. Alexander acidly
suggested he look, and finally some were found. The Long
Bridge, offering direct contact with Arlington, seemed the best
tended of the three, but even there Alexander concluded that
the sixty-four-man guard could not be expected to repulse a
determined attack. All bridges required better fire protection,
and the first two needed boats attached to the defending forces
in order to secure against incendiaries getting at the inflam-
mable undersides.[23]

Everywhere Halleck looked, decay and demoralization characterized the Washington defenses—even the earthworks
showed scrub growth and tall grass on supposedly cleared fields
of fire.

Sunday, July 10, passed as a fearsomely long day. Rumors of the enemy were heard from several scouting parties, but real information did not come until nearly five in the afternoon. When it came, it came from frighteningly close by:

> Washington Road,
> Two miles from Rockville,
> July 10, 1864—4 P.M.

Maj. Gen. C. C. Augur:

General: I have taken position and formed. My rear guard is fighting the enemy near Rockville. I have been joined by a squadron Eighth Illinois Cavalry and expect to be engaged in a few moments. I would respectfully suggest that the forts in the vicinity of Tennallytown be strongly guarded as the enemy's column is a mile long.

Very respectfully, your obedient servant,

> Wm. H. Fry,
> *Major, Commanding.*[24]

The entire city had suffered alarms during the Sabbath; high command had been confused, overlapped, and almost useless; stragglers and refugees continued to crowd in, along with assorted herds of cattle driven from Early's tender mercies. The city had virtually surrendered to terror before the Rebels reached the ramparts. Now that the enemy was at hand, the only voice of calm to be heard in the babel of panic was Lincoln's. To an hysterical group of Baltimore citizens who had the affrontery to wonder if they could count on the President for full protection, he offered a typical suggestion: "Let us be vigilant, but keep cool. I hope neither Baltimore nor Washington will be taken." [25]

6

---- * ----

REBELS AT THE RAMPARTS

TIME, one of man's most ingenious conceptions, measures human endeavor and so gives meaning to history. Without it, life would be a pointless coagulation of experience. Now and then time has almost mystic properties which capture briefly a cleavage between past and future and arrest for history some fateful moment. Mostly these moments go unrecognized until later, but there are occasions when time's dimension subtly changes, when life looms larger, when light and shade take sharper hue, when men move in a strange knowledge of great deeds.

Around Washington on the morning of July 11, 1864, things seemed measured in this different time; what happened in the next few hours would alter history. All the bloody decisions of three long years, all the death and destruction, counted now for practically nothing. For the Confederacy, Washington lay a glittering prize, one which might convince the world of Southern invincibility. And the prize would fall to Early's hands if his tired army reached the city's defenses before more Yankees came up from the South. History suddenly came down to a small segment on the face of a clock: time became both the ultimate weapon and the final arbiter.

For Jubal Early, July 11 began in a hurry. Gruelling heat the previous day had exacted a toll from his infantry and he knew it; the long night had been oppressively hot and most of the men had slept poorly. Excitement probably had something to do with it, but heat had been the main cause of insomnia. Lack of sleep certainly would slow the army's pace in the morning, but Early determined to push ahead as swiftly as he could manage. Sandie Pendleton, reporting to headquarters on the previous evening, copied Jubal's marching order for Monday:

> Headquarters Valley District,
> July 10, 1864.

Major-General Breckinridge, Commanding, &c.:

General: The following is the order of march for to-morrow: First, Rodes' division moves in advance at 3.30 A.M. General Long will send a battery of artillery to follow his advance brigade, and the rest of the battalion of artillery will follow the division. Second, Ramseur follows this battalion of artillery. General Long will send another battalion after him. Third, Gordon follows next after the second battalion of Long's artillery. Fourth, the wagon trains come next, and fifth, the rear is to be brought up by Echols' division, which will be accompanied by Colonel King's battalion of artillery, one battery coming just in rear of the last brigade.

By order of Lieutenant-General Early:

> A. S. Pendleton,
> *Assistant Adjutant-General.*[1]

If all went according to Early's hopes, his infantry might storm the Washington works before nightfall, enter the enemy's capital and there wait for Bradley Johnson—if Johnson made it to the rendezvous at Point Lookout. Surely a big if, but Early had no time to worry about contingencies and frightening pos-

sibilities. Before daylight he rose, mounted and rode forward
to see that the camps were alerted, the men moving. Quickly
the men finished hasty breakfasts, struck camps, slung on
haversacks, and took to the road. Before sunup all of Early's
columns were en route, long, ghostly lines snaking southeastward. Ahead he had sent McCausland to probe for roaming
Yankee cavalry encountered the day before, but resistance remained light. About midmorning Early rode into Rockville
and stopped to confer with some of his commanders. Orders
were checked, clearly understood. McCausland would stick to
the main pike at Rockville that would take him east-southeast
toward the Tennallytown approaches to Washington. The infantry, Rodes still leading, would take the left fork at Rockville and aim for Silver Spring and Bladensburg. At Silver
Spring the infantry would turn sharply to the right and march
down the Seventh Street Road—one of Washington's main
arteries. McCausland would keep headquarters well informed
about developing enemy defense, and General Long would see
to it that artillery remained close to front elements.

Early watched as the gray columns trudged through Rockville. Doubtless he saw with rising concern the fatigue which
etched so many faces, the sore-footed gait of hardened soldiers.
"No air stirring," he noted, the day "an exceedingly hot one."
At times he could scarcely make out the men through the dust
billowing along the lines.[2] Heat, dust, sweat—all these were
special hazards to marches, but they were more special today
than ever in Early's recollection. Stragglers increased, men lay
down by the roadside, but still he urged officers to push the
column.

Jubal rode slowly along his infantry and finally stopped at a
temporary vantage point near Rockville. McCausland spurred
to him with satisfying intelligence: enemy cavalry alone harassed the van and it seemed likely there would be no severe

interference on the Georgetown road. Breckinridge rode up
from the rear of the column to report that Federal horsemen
were now keeping their distance behind the Army of the Valley. Early talked earnestly to Breckinridge and McCausland,
and the three waited to hear from Rodes about the infantry's
fortunes. Midday passed, with heat intensifying as tension
mounted. Finally, around 1 P.M., loud, heavy explosions were
heard from the direction of Washington. Siege ordnance!
Everyone knew what that meant; the Confederate advance had
come within range of the Washington works.

Now came the hardest part of the day. With firing in front,
Early desperately wanted to ride ahead and supervise the field.
But he knew that the most important thing now was to close
his columns so that he could present maximum force at the
enemy's ramparts. Closing the columns would not be easy. The
number of stragglers dropping back grew during the passing
afternoon; the lines thinned out until one of Gordon's old
soldiers observed that "our division was stretched out almost
like skirmishers." [3] Early rode along the weary regiments,
urging, cajoling, threatening—Close up, close up. But men
could do just so much; those who clung grimly to the march
did so at a dragging pace. Jubal tried a new tack: he galloped
up and down the columns talking of Washington and saying
he would have the men in the enemy's capital by nightfall. But
even that news failed to spark his parched and jaded legions:
they would get there when they got there—more speed was
simply beyond them. [4]

As he looked at them, those thin, incredibly spent men, an
awful fact bore in on Jubal: if time still worked for him, nature
worked against him. Climate and geography were beyond the
powers of a commanding general. If he won the race with time,
he might lose the match to temperature.

Swiftly, a desperate excitement spurring him on, Early gal-

loped ahead of the infantry and joined a small detachment of
cavalry which he urged along the Seventh Street road beyond
Silver Spring. A few blue-coated cavalry fought the Confederate advance without success and finally fell back to the cover
of heavy works on the Seventh Street pike. Early watched as
his horsemen skillfully swung from their saddles, fanned out
into a curtain of skirmishers, and efficiently probed the enemy
front. What was the situation? As far as Jubal could tell, things
looked favorable. From a point of vantage he examined the
enemy works with his glasses. Ahead of him about 1,100 yards
away loomed a large earthen work, curtained, scarped, em-
brasured. Early unrolled the large map of Washington's defenses that Jed Hotchkiss had prepared, located Seventh Street
road and saw that he was looking at Fort Stevens, a major work
designed to protect the vital highway leading to the heart of
Washington. The fort stood to the right of the road and was
elevated slightly. Between Jubal's lookout and the fort were
clumps of trees, occasional farmhouses, cleared fields. The
trend of terrain was downward toward a little stream which
formed a small vale in front of Fort Stevens.

At the moment Early paid little attention to details of
ground: was Fort Stevens occupied? Yes, but as he looked,
Early saw that few figures stood against the sky. Manned, but
feebly manned, was Fort Stevens, and that told a promising
story: surely the enemy knew the direction of Confederate
advance and had concentrated all available strength against it.
If Fort Stevens had few defenders, there were few defenders
for all of Washington. Jubal had beaten the clock; he had out-
marched Grant, and in front lay the greatest prize ever offered
to an American soldier! All he had to do was organize a line
and occupy the works.

But organizing a line proved almost impossible. Scarcely
more than 10,000 weary Rebels were still with the army, and

of these not more than a third could be considered fit for immediate duty. Early found Robert Rodes leading his men down the pike from Silver Spring. Throw out skirmishers, ordered Jubal, deploy a line of battle and see if the works could be taken. Rodes did his best to obey, but his men were strewn out on the road in flank order and all he could do for some time was fan his skirmishers into the fields in front of the Yankee lines. While Rodes pushed his men as well as circumstances would permit, Early still at his vantage point, kept swinging his glasses along the Union positions. Suddenly about one-thirty [5] he noticed a pall of dust lofting over Washington. What did it signify? Reinforcements probably. Hand to the brim of his old slouch hat, Jubal looked long and hard and at length saw a column of bluecoats swing into view. The Yanks were marching resolutely for the fortifications. No locals these; the uniforms told the story. The home units and local militia had been decked, some of them, in linen dusters,[6] but these men wore the faded blues of old campaigners. They were some of Grant's men. How many were there? Was there time yet to carry the lines ere all of the VIth Union Corps arrived?

Answers to these questions Early could obtain only by careful reconnaissance, and reconnaissance would burn daylight! No help for it. Rodes received orders to probe the lines near Fort Stevens, and Early rode along the lines toward the right. What news did McCausland have? Perhaps the enemy had stripped all the works to the South so as to present a bold front at Fort Stevens. But a report from the cavalry leader dashed that hope: works near the Georgetown pike were too strongly held for assault.[7] Any sort of information from inside the city about enemy numbers would have been welcome, and Early had some hope that Southern sympathizers in Washington would sneak through the lines with data about reinforcements. But if there were any Southern adherents there, they were distinguished by their absence. Even trusted John Mosby, asked to find out what happened near the capital, had failed to report, although he did his best to work close to Georgetown.[8] Nothing for it but to rely on Rodes' exploration of his front.

Gray skirmishers sprinted forward toward the Federal lines, shoving bluecoats ahead of them. Enemy skirmish opposition was at first more heroic than effective. Early and the blue-eyed Rodes watched as the Rebel skirmish line drew near the enemy entrenchments and noted the sudden eddies of smoke from new batteries. Late in the day more bluecoats joined the skirmish line and fought with veteran coolness. A close look at the whole front about sundown made a lasting impression on Jubal. The works he saw were

> exceedingly strong, and consisted of what appeared to be enclosed forts for heavy artillery, with a tier of lower works in front of each pierced for an immense number of guns, the whole being connected by curtains and ditches in front, and strengthened by palisades and abattis. The timber had been felled within cannon range all around and left on the ground, making a formidable obstacle, and every possible approach was raked by artillery. On the [Confederate] right was Rock Creek, running through a deep ravine which had been rendered impassable by the felling of the timber on each side, and beyond were the works on the Georgetown pike which had been reported to be the strongest of all. On the left, as far as the eye could reach, the works appeared to be of the same impregnable character. The position was naturally strong for defence, and the examination showed, what might have been expected, that every appliance of science and unlimited means had been used to render the fortifications around Washington as strong as possible.[9]

Early's hopes began to fade. His natural combativeness had to yield to caution in face of such strength. The only chance now lay in the possibility that Federal reinforcements were few. But that seemed unlikely. Still, the Army of the Valley had come too far, General Lee had risked too much, for Early to retire from Washington without making a try for it. Concerned and thoughtful, Jubal left Rodes' men at the front and turned his mount toward Silver Spring. About two miles from his skirmish line, he came to the handsome home of Francis P. Blair. Energetic Kyd Douglas had put a guard on the house and saved it for Jubal's headquarters. Here, in the evening, the commanding general called a council of war.

Rodes, Ramseur, Breckinridge, and Gordon assembled and found the General playing host with more than usual gusto. Fortunately for them, the Blair wine cellar still boasted a few bottles saved by Douglas' squad of guards, and as the officers debated the future they toasted the present.[10] Breckinridge recalled many previous times when, as Vice-President of the United States, he had been a guest in the house and sipped various vintages at the behest of friend Blair. Early soon brought the meeting to the immediate problem: What should the army do? Would an attack on Washington be worth the risk? Think of the prospect of reinstalling Breckinridge in the vice-presidential chair! That alone seemed to justify a fling at the forts in the morning.

And aside from that happy possibility, Early reminded his cohorts of all the reasons for the campaign, the stake the Confederacy had in the presence of the army before Washington, and added an ominous warning: Hunter was known to be closing on the rear of the Army of the Valley, and if the army dawdled too long, the passes of South Mountain and the Potomac Fords would be sealed tight. Considerable debate followed Jubal's questions; not all of the assembled brass agreed on what ought to be done,[11] but Early's aggressive spirit and innate

distrust of subordinates' advice, forced him to a decision. He
would attack at dawn, "unless some information should be
received before that time showing its impractibility [*sic*]." [12]

The information came in the form of intelligence from
Bradley Johnson. He reported exciting exploits. Not yet at
Point Lookout, he was still pushing toward it. His men had
been in the saddle now for almost sixty-seven hours, had
circled northward and struck the Northern Central Railroad
at Cockeysville, and a detachment had destroyed the Philadelphia, Wilmington, and Baltimore RR bridge on the
Gunpowder River. The same detachment had captured several
trains and prisoners, and among the prisoners had been Major
General William B. Franklin, famed of the Army of the
Potomac. The Federal general finally escaped because Johnson's men were so tired that they slept while he ran. But
Johnson had entered Baltimore county, sent out scouts to
Baltimore and now had learned that two Federal army corps
were moving to support Washington. Until he had other orders,
Johnson would continue toward Point Lookout. [13]

Two Federal corps? Early knew of the VIth, but rumor now
had it that the XIXth, fresh from the Red River fiasco in
Louisiana, had almost arrived in the Union capital. One corps
of hardened veterans gave pause, two would mean that an
attack on the formidable works must be called off. Until he
could be certain of the odds, Early decided to suspend attack
orders. With daylight he would reconnoiter the lines. [14]

Essentially Johnson's information had been accurate. Across
the skirmish lines during the afternoon of the eleventh some
significant alterations in the status of Washington occurred.
The morning had crept by with General Chris Augur, General
A. D. McCook, Halleck, Secretary Stanton and the President
in a state of perplexity. Despite the fact that cavalry pickets

made contact with the Rebels early in the day, no reasonable estimates of Early's strength could be made. If Wallace's figure of 20,000 were correct, the city probably would be taken before the remainder of the VI Corps arrived. Some still argued there were far fewer Rebels at hand than the hysterical War Department imagined, but at least one picket warned that 100,000 Confederates were at the gates, led by none other than General Lee himself! [15]

In the crisis of the longest morning Washington had known, few were idle. But the very frenzy of activity nullified much that ought to have been done. East of the Seventh Street pike and not far from the earthworks, the President kept the summer White House open, much to the alarm of Stanton and the presidential guard of Pennsylvanians. From there Lincoln persisted in riding to the front lines, and his carriage wandered around alarmingly. It seemed especially dangerous since the Rebel elements were growing bold, and might well take occasion to do harm to a Chief Executive who loved to slip his guards. Stanton finally ordered him to get back to the White House. One thing could be said for the President—he did not interfere with what defense measures apparently were underway. He did worry about what ought to be done and was not, and had curtly commented on the shortage of troops to Grant. [16] And of all officials within the besieged capital—for besieged it was—Lincoln seemed the only one who thought in offensive terms. He felt the Rebels could be thrown back well enough, but he wanted them wrecked. Early should not be allowed to escape south of the Potomac. Grant had agreed, and had sent the rest of the VI Corps to Washington and made arrangements for a 6,000-man division of the XIX Corps to proceed directly from Fort Monroe to Washington. Beyond that he could do no more.

But while the city waited for help from Grant, local com-

manders continued to confound confusion. There were far too
many generals milling about, and a snarl developed over the
command responsibility of Augur and Halleck's favorite,
Quincy Gillmore. McCook had some sort of authority over the
forts in the northern defense perimeter, but even he could not
define it. Troops still marched around in a maze of conflicting
orders, and all kinds of units continued to take arms. And
amid the scenes of creeping desperation, Montgomery Meigs
at last received his summons to glory. "Meigs' division" of
quartermaster employees went to the field. Unfortunately they
had a little trouble finding it, but they went. Some of the old
companies—not mustered for months—which had forgotten
what little they once had known of martial maneuvering,
wandered around aimlessly, and at least one of General Dan
Rucker's units of employees from his extensive Washington
Depot misinterpreted an order. Directed to report to Rucker's
headquarters—transferred from the Depot to the vicinity of
Fort Totten—they marched away from the front and reported
to his old established headquarters at the Washington Quartermaster Depot! [17]

Just how bad things were some could guess by the activity
at many of the city's banks. These citadels of caution were
scenes of feverish activity; currency, bonds, all sorts of valu-
ables were being packed for hasty shipment down the Potomac.
The pitiful huddles of refugees continued to pour into the
streets and added theirs to the ever-swelling stock of rumors.
Extras were issued by the city's papers, but offered nothing
reliable about the state of the capital—all that was known for
sure was that there were Rebels at the ramparts. The composure
which usually marked the citizenry had begun to unravel when
Lew Wallace had abandoned the front at the Monocacy. And
when the cannon boomed from the northwest, the horror of
war struck home.

A little after noon [18] sporadic cheering could be heard at the Sixth Street docks. Crowds gathered hastily as transports began pulling in and discharging thick clouds of bluecoats. Here was a division of the Old Sixth Corps, men renowned on many a bloody Virginia field. Often in past years the city had seen the guidons and patches marked with the Greek Cross, but never had the Sixth Corps insignia looked so good! Another division would land in the morning, and 650 men of the XIX Corps were on hand. With some 10,000 old hands in the defenses, Rebel general, Early, would have his work cut out for him.

At the head of the troops as they debarked came General Horatio Wright. Orders from Halleck greeted him and started his men on the wrong road out toward Georgetown. Recalled and redirected, they headed for the Seventh Street road and the vicinity of Fort Stevens.[19] To the harried Halleck, and equally harried Augur, the VI Corps had an importance beyond its numbers: many of its men had mustered in Washington, had received early training on the big guns of the forts, and could replace the amateurs who at that very moment struggled to learn how to ram powder and shell.[20]

Horatio Wright brought a different spirit to the defense of Washington. As soon as he knew where the fighting was, he rode ahead of his men and reported to McCook at Fort Stevens. There he saw skirmishers in action and made a quick survey of the field. The Rebel line looked thin, thin enough not to be badly hurt by the heavy ordnance in the fort. If the Southerners were disposed to shake out a thin curtain, they deserved to have it smashed. But McCook, whose beleaguered Ohio militia had done credit to the regulars that day, could not make the decision—he thought the question of attack had been left in Augur's charge.

Swiftly Wright scrawled a request to the department com-

mander, asking permission to "clean out" the Rebel skirmishers. "General McCook's men," he said, "are not as good
as mine for this purpose." While he wrote, firing could be heard
spreading along the rim of Federal works farther to the left
—Forts Reno, Kearney and Simmons were embattled. Perhaps
a general Rebel assault would start soon, and engage a substantial portion of the thirty-seven-mile Union line. If so,
Wright wanted the initial advantage of a field clear of enemy
skirmishers, and should all enemy activity be merely a demonstration, a sharp check of the gray advance lines might expose
the fact. Here was a soldier's idea, but it seemed too daring
to the defensive-minded garrison. Augur, still afraid that his
front could not be held, thought it imprudent to attack and
answered: "I do not consider it advisable to make any advance
until our lines are better established." [21]

If Wright chafed at such timidity, he must have fumed at
orders which soon reached him: hold the VI Corps in reserve,
directed Halleck, move it into line only in case of attack.
Meanwhile, the front would be left in charge of the lame, halt,
and blind! And when the veterans from the Deep South, the
van of the XIX Corps, arrived, they were to file right and take
up positions near Fort Saratoga, where the enemy had yet to
threaten. Such idiocy could not be tolerated, and at length
Wright received grudging permission to go to the front. When
his lead elements reached Fort Stevens the situation had
deteriorated; the Federal skirmish line of Ohioans, Veteran
Reserves, War Department clerks, and citizen volunteers had
started to give way, and Early's men were almost in the fort.

Wright wasted no time. Brigadier General Frank Wheaton
received quick instructions: take 500 men of the First Brigade
of the Second Division forward at once and recover the original
skirmish line! And while the 98th, 102nd, and 139th Pennsylvania Veteran Volunteers waded into the evening skirmish

which so impressed Early, Fort Stevens became a grandstand seat for a curious assemblage of citizens. Gideon Welles, acid Navy Secretary, watched some of the fighting, and with an irritating shrewdness asked where the main enemy force was. No one seemed to know; Wright and McCook ventured that Early's main body probably lurked a mile or so away. "I asked why their whereabouts was not ascertained, and their strength known. The reply was that we had no fresh cavalry." [22]

Another, even more distinguished kibitzer visited the fort while skirmish fire rattled. President Lincoln, again giving vent to his curiosity, appeared and took a look over the parapet. His presence was noted by a combat artist from *Frank Leslie's Weekly,* who constructed a sketch of the long-limbed Chief Executive mounted on a horse watching the shooting. [23]

For Lincoln and other viewers, the scene had all the horrors of a great battle. The fields in front of the fort crawled with blue infantry; and on the Rebel hills opposite, gathering twilight was broken by the fire-flecks of hundreds of muskets and the licking flames of burning houses. The houses, set ablaze by Fort Stevens' guns, had been Rebel sharpshooters' nests and had to be eliminated. There, in tiny tableau, was life, death, fire and destruction—war in microcosm. Finally the grayclads pulled back, and the skirmish lines secured for the night—a night disturbed by nervous firing on the tense picket lines.

If sleep eluded the men in the lines, it eluded most of Washington that night. The city was an armed camp, alert, dreading, expectant.

Across the lines, Early's army slept fairly well. Whatever the old man planned would be revealed all too soon. And whatever chanced on the morrow, old soldiers knew they could better meet it after a night's rest.

If Jubal slept well—and he usually did—he did not sleep

long. As soon as there was light on the eastern horizon Tuesday morning, Jube swung into the saddle and rode for the front. Atop a small hill, he looked long and carefully at the enemy's forts and rifle pits. What he saw would dictate the action of the Army of the Valley on the twelfth of July.

A good many of Washington's loyal citizens had a similar feeling that the Army of the Valley would dictate what happened to them that day. Still, although "the sun rose upon a day of excitement," as one observer recalled, there seemed an indefinable sense of relief in the air. The enemy still sieged the gates, but the battle-hardened men from Grant looked like they could handle the situation. Excitement now had more of anticipation than fear to it; people caught the thrill of danger, and many wanted to go to the front. Crowds of the idly curious began to choke the Seventh Street pike, and the Military Governor of Washington established Provost Marshal guards to hold back all those without proper passes.

Curious how many were able to procure authority to get to the front, despite urgent military need for the avenues to the northwest. Governor Moses Wisewell did his best, but the sheer bulk of sightseers almost got beyond him. Those who braved possible official wrath for a chance to sniff gunpowder soon learned that there were Confederates everywhere. Reports from scouts sent out during the previous evening indicated that the Rebel's right flank rested on the Potomac, above Tennallytown, and their line swung concavely around to the B&O tracks near Bladensburg. If true, there were thousands of them, and the day promised to be exciting indeed. One further item of exciting intelligence: Washington had been isolated from the rest of the Union, rail lines cut, telegraph connection severed. Tuesday the city would chart its own fate.[24]

Morning passed without incident. Even the quarrelsome

skirmishers quit their sniping and basked in the summer sun. The Union garrison lazed behind parapets; the Rebels shaded themselves in surrounding woodland. Casual observers would hardly have noticed war around Washington.

To alert Federal officers, the long silence must have been extremely revealing, and highly satisfying. Considering all the known factors, Jube Early's failure to assault at dawn probably could be taken as sure evidence he did not intend to make a serious try for the Federal capital. Each passing moment gave him less time to attack, occupy, and escape, and a canny opponent like Old Jube could be counted on to know that the odds against him were mounting.

If any of the blue brass reasoned along those lines, they would have been right. Early's moment of decision had come almost with dawn.

As it grew light near the Union entrenchments, Jube strained to count the figures looming along the lines. If there were no more than the night before . . . even if there were a few more . . . he would fight for Washington if there was any chance at all of success. General Lee expected the Army of the Valley to do everything possible to reap the rewards of the offensive-defensive. Early knew that Grant had already reacted to the strategy by detaching two corps; what would the loss of Washington, even temporarily, force "the Hammerer" to do? While he ran his glasses slowly along the front, Early pondered the basic essential of Grant vs. Lee, and certain other questions of immediate concern.

If he attacked and broke into the city, how many Union reserves would he find? As far as Early could estimate, he had about 9,000 infantry and possibly 1,000 troopers on hand. Furious, house-to-house combat would sap manpower, reduce Confederate strength so sharply that the remnant of the Valley

Army might be sealed up in Washington and captured in toto.
Then there was the question of the Point Lookout prisoners.
Apparently he might just as well cease to worry about them,
though; reports indicated the enemy had wind of efforts afoot
to free them and had doubled vigilance in the immediate area.
While that removed one concern, it posed another: what of
Bradley Johnson and his men? If Washington were occupied,
Johnson might rejoin the army via the Bladensburg road. If
the city were not taken, and Early lost the battle, Johnson's
command, too, might be captured.

Each of these questions had to be weighed, and above them
all loomed so vast a consideration that Early hardly dared
think of it. Should Washington fall, even for a short time,
diplomatic recognition of the Confederacy might well follow
—a possibility that elated Confederates and chilled some
Washington officials! [25]

Now the sun was up, shadows fading from the enemy ramparts. The dusty trees cast a bit of shade, but the fields were
clearly in view, and across the little ravine guns glinted brightly.
Fort Stevens, the rifle pits stretching west to Fort De Russy and
east to Fort Slocum, the batteries and embrasures—all were
filled with blue uniforms! In the gentle summer breeze, a banner flapped lackadaisically: was that the Greek Cross? Probably, for the "faded coats of blue" showed the men to be
veteran soldiers. And more must be coming; there were dust
eddies back over the city. [26]

General Lee had worried about some of Jubal Early's traits,
and hoped some might be modified. Jube was impetuous, apt
to commit his men too hastily without adequate reconnaissance
and without waiting for full concentration. But independent
command often works its own changes in a man, and Early
had learned a lot about war since the night of June 12, when
Lee had given him Stonewall's Corps. It was a month to the

day since Jubal assumed command of the new Army of the Valley, a short while on the calendar, but an era in the tempering of a general. He still loved to fight, and his tobacco cud worked furiously as his battle spirit raged. He wanted to hurl infantry forward; above all he wanted his beloved batteries to open and clear the enemy from his front.

A month ago Major General Early, commanding a division, would have given the orders. Today, Lieutenant General Early, commanding a Confederate field army, would not. The odds, he regretted to admit, were all against him in an attack. He must order the men to hold the front and plan his retreat. Obviously a retreat at night was the better part of bravery—there were more Yanks across the way than Early's small force could handle in a fighting retreat. Too, a stand for a day would lend credence and strength to the threat against Washington, and would give Bradley Johnson a chance to get back to the army. Speed a courier to Johnson at once with orders to return.[27] Deploy skirmishers along the two miles from Fort Slocum to Fort De Russy; organize Gordon and Rodes in lines of battle against the possiblity of an enemy sortie. Order McCausland to keep the Yankees busy on the Georgetown pike. Beyond that, wait for the cover of night.

Fortunately for the Confederates, Union defenders were happy to wait. Some of the green militiamen still in Fort Stevens watched with mounting terror as Rodes and Gordon threw out their skirmishers, and followed with long lines of battle. Old soldiers noted, though, that the battle lines stayed far back of the van, and were not in attack formation. When the gray-clads lay down in woods and thickets, the whole front settled to an occasional snarl of picket and artillery fire.[28] Save for the rare puffs of smoke, Washington's defenses lay tranquil and shimmered in the mounting heat.

While Wright and some of his brigadiers chafed that no one

seemed anxious to force any sort of decision, Halleck and Augur feverishly worked at getting more men into the defenses. The District of Columbia militia they were still trying to mobilize and more government clerks were urged forward. And through all this milling humanity, sightseers once again clogged the road to the front. Those fortunates who had passes discovered that merely getting to the forts involved no little heroism. One would-be onlooker, Lucius Chittenden, a fairly high official in the U.S. Treasury Department, later recalled the troubles he and friends endured en route to Fort Stevens that afternoon:

We managed to procure passes and to drive out to Fort Stevens about 4 oclock P.M. Regulations had been adopted prohibiting citizens from going to the front. We left Willard's Hotel about 3½ oclock driving out on the Seventh St Road. We passed a large number of the 6th Corps on the march. As we drove into the open fields in order to avoid the columns we encountered many soldiers in the lively stage of drunkenness all armed with loaded muskets. The transit was any thing but pleasant. Arriving at the summit of Meridian hill, beyond boundary Street, we found a multitude of citizens who were not permitted to go beyond that point. Although the Sentinel insisted with many oaths that he could not pass any one in the dress of a Citizen, beyond that point, no matter by whom his pass was signed, I succeeded in reasoning him into an exception in our favor under Gov Wisewells pass, and we went our way. From this place to Fort Stevens we saw few citizens. I may say almost none. But we pased many Regiments and Companies of veteran troops. Here upon one side in a field of standing corn was the baggage train of a Regiment, the mules enjoying the luxury of green forage—on the other side, perhaps the shelter tents of the men were pitched in an oat field just ready for the sickle— The comfort of man and horse was evidently first consulted—the interest of the farmer was made a matter of secondary consideration. I am obliged to confess moreover that the remarks of the soldiers upon my equipage were not always of the most civil character. These remarks were in this wise, always answered by us in good temper however and we usually disarmed our assailants. 'You are non combatants, You are!' 'Coming out here to get up another Bull run ar'nt ye?' 'Skedaddle white livers!' &c &c. . . . On we went past Regiment and division, through the first and second toll gates, passing picket after picket until at length we came to Fort Stevens.[20]

And by the time Chittenden and his party reached the fort, General Wright and General McCook had come to a conclusion. During most of the day, Rebel skirmishers had been creeping closer to the Union positions, and their work was made easier for them by the fact that two houses still standing across the ravine offered cover to sharpshooters. These sharp-eyed riflemen picked off numbers of bluecoats as they disputed the skirmishers' advance. The houses must be eliminated, and in addition, two little knolls commanding a section of the Federal rifle pits must be captured. If the Southerners could be driven from the woods and houses, Fort Stevens would be a far safer place for such citizens as Chittenden and Gideon Welles—the Navy chief again peered over the trenches and made his acrid mental notes. Preparations to carry the objectives were carefully made in the early afternoon, preparations confounded no little by the civilians who were somehow still slipping through the Provost Marshal guards!

While General Wheaton, temporarily commanding George Getty's Second Division of the VI Corps, brought up the men he wanted for the attack, Wright and McCook decided to survey the potential battlefield. As he stepped from his headquarters at Fort Stevens, Wright ran into the President of the United States, once again out for a look at the war. Wright queried whether Mr. Lincoln would care to view the scene of action, "without for a moment supposing he would accept." Yes. And suddenly Wright saw to his horror that Lincoln had joined a group atop the fort's parapet. From the two sharp-shooter roosts across the lines came the heavy bang of long range rifles and lead whistled around the sightseers. Wright, standing next to the President, urged Lincoln to get down—if he were killed, the cause might well go with him. But still the tall figure in the stovepipe hat looked out on the battlefield. A thud, and one of the men near Lincoln clutched his thigh, started to keel over, and was helped off the wall.

A few observers saw the earnest conversation going on between Wright and Lincoln under Confederate fire, but most of the men in the fort were too busy to pay much attention. Not far from the General and the President, however, a young officer took a moment's rest, glanced up, saw a tall civilian idiotically showing himself to Rebel rifles and yelled "Get down, you fool." [30]

Apparently amused at the brash words of young Captain Oliver Wendell Holmes, Lincoln at last heeded the increasingly peremptory urgings of Wright and clambered down from the wall.

Now General Wright could get on with military business.[31] General Wheaton received orders to go ahead. He in turn called on the Third Brigade, under Colonel Dan Bidwell, to deploy and follow skirmishers forward. About five-thirty every-thing was ready. Wheaton instructed Bidwell that he should move his men up under cover as far as possible, keeping them at trail arms so that the fading sun would not glint on their gun barrels; when formed behind the skirmishers, a signal would be given, ordnance would open from Fort Stevens and the assault could begin. Problems of terrain facing the would-be attackers were best described by Lucius Chittenden. Thoroughly a civilian, Chittenden remembered the scene in its every detail:

Standing on the embankment [slightly east of Fort Stevens and just behind Union rifle pits] we were in view of the whole field, which was spread out like a panorama. From that point to the crest of the hill near Blair's house, the distance could not be less than two miles. The field sloped gently down from our defenses to the brook a distance of something over a half mile and rose with a similar grade to the crest about 1½ mile further. This brought the opposite slope of the hill into full view from our position.

Directly in front of Ft Stevens the slope toward the brook was nearly bare of vegetation. Crossing the brook was a fine wooden mansion two stories in height, with a cupola, the residence of Mr Lay of the P.O. Dept. A little beyond was the chimney of a house burned by our shells the day before. A small space around these houses was cleared, and then came a wide tract covered with a growth of oak brushwood from 6, to 15 ft in height. Beyond this again was a large wheat field at the farther side of which was a strip of large forest trees. On the corner near 7th St Road was the residence of Mr Roach.

In front of . . . [the embankment] and sweeping around to the right was a large open space from which the timber had been just removed, and the stumps left standing. On a slight elevation a few rods from the Rifle pits was a recently constructed earth work. To the left of this was a peach orchard in front of that a field of growing corn, then an open soace to the brook. In this space a few large trees were left standing.

Across the brook was another field smaller in extent but covered with brush similar to that on the opposite side of the road. Through this starting from a point in the 7th St Road just beyond the brook a bridle path led to a residence, standing on the crest of the hill at some distance west [east] from the highway. This was surrounded by a large meadow and cultivated grounds. . . . Farther still and just at the top of the rise was a large forest of original growth.[32]

Facing this difficult ground, Bidwell's men did well enough
in getting into position. At around 6 P.M., the signal was given,
Fort Steven's embrasures spat flame and were wreathed in
heavy white smoke. As soon as shells began to erupt in the
Rebel lines, Federal skirmishers leaped forward, and Bidwell's
lines of battle followed. A ripping sound came from the Confederate trees, a solid sheet of flame burst in front of the
Federal infantry, the ranks reeled, gaps appeared, file closers
did their best, and Bidwell called for supporting regiments.
His men had surprised the enemy, but had in turn been surprised. Instead of striking a thin line of Rebel pickets, they
had blundered on a line of battle. Reinforcements up, the
attack resumed against stiffening opposition. More bluecoats
were summoned and the Rebels retired, but nightfall stalled
progress. Winking gunflashes continued until about 10 P.M.,
and then all grew quiet. The hills which Wright and McCook
so wanted had been won at a cost of about 250 men.[33] The
distinguished guests in the Fort Stevens bleachers saw a sight
far more satisfying than the Federal rout at First Bull Run
that a similar Washington audience witnessed on another July
day in 1861.

The line of battle which had surprised Bidwell had been
constructed by Rodes. The Yankee assault had come in
sterner measure than anticipated. Rodes had called for more
of his division, and for a brief time in the twilight it looked as
though a major battle was under way—a battle Early might
not be able to break off. When Kyd Douglas saw the Yanks
start forward, he thought "we were 'gone up.' "[34] And he was
not alone! Lots of Rebels were suddenly scared, and when
the firing died away in the darkness thousands heaved inaudible
sighs of relief.

Jubal had not been idle. He trusted his subordinates to hold
a disputed field, and had been busying himself with getting

ready to leave Washington. Everything looked bad by dark. McCausland fought a steadily losing action on the extreme right, and, with the unexpected aggressiveness of the enemy center, Early knew his decision to pull out was eminently correct. Johnson, if he could cut his way back, would have to join the army on the retreat.[35] To be certain that everyone knew what would be the line of march, Early asked Breckinridge and Gordon to visit headquarters, and they came after dark. Firing still echoed in the woods, the heavy reverberation of a big shell occasionally shook the ground, but they all knew by then that they would get away. Early called for his friend Kyd Douglas, whose humor Jubal vastly appreciated. When the major reported, Early dispensed first with business: to cover the retreat a picket line must be left behind; it would consist of 200 men and officers, and Douglas would stay with the pickets until after midnight unless ordered or driven away. After midnight, Douglas would retire as a rear guard until supplanted by cavalry. Just as the young Marylander arose to discharge his rather fearsome duty, Early called to him: "Major, we haven't taken Washington, but we've scared Abe Lincoln like hell!"

At that particular moment Douglas' vaunted sense of humor was a little strained, and he answered acidly: "Yes, General, but this afternoon when that Yankee line moved out against us, I think some other people were scared blue as hell's brimstone!" Breckinridge guffawed, and broke in: "How about that, General?" "That's true," Early piped in his high falsetto, "but it won't appear in history!" [36]

Take the lead, Early told Breckinridge, and push the march. Ramseur and Rodes would follow as soon as possible, and the frazzled cavalry would try to hold back pursuit.

As things turned out, pursuit was fairly feeble—Washington's defenders appeared too relieved to press Early's men.

The Second Massachusetts Cavalry did make trouble during the early hours of the thirteenth, but Johnson's ragged regiments, which returned from their expedition after midnight, dispersed the hostile horsemen and the retreat continued.[37] Early took the army to Rockville, turned the columns southwestward toward White's Ford. Hectic marches still lay ahead, but the infantry kept up the old pace of the Army of the Valley; supply officers worked like fiends to garner as much food and as many horses as possible, and did a good job of keeping the trains closed. Through Poolesville the long gray lines passed and reached White's Ford about midnight of July 13–14. During the morning of the fourteenth the Army of the Valley crossed the Potomac, and by evening went into camp near Leesburg—the contributions levied on Hagerstown and Frederick, all the prisoners taken at the Battle of Monocacy, all the captured livestock, were safely out of enemy clutches.

Two things about the expedition worried Early at this moment, one major and one minor. First, the hard marching and almost continuous skirmishing had taken a toll of Jubal's thin ranks. The cost of scaring Abe Lincoln ran to about 2,000 men. He had started with 12,000. There had been much straggling, of course, so some of the "missing" might conceivably turn up later. Second, as the army had moved out of the enemy's country, some Confederate, without Early's knowledge or authorization, had apparently set fire to the home of U.S. Postmaster General Montgomery Blair—not far from the Francis Blair house which had served as Jubal's headquarters. Early thought the act entirely justifiable in view of Hunter's earlier depredations in the Shenandoah, but he regretted the incident. And he regretted, too, that Bradley Johnson had taken it on himself to burn the home of Governor A. W. Bradford of Maryland. Questions of discipline aside, this sort of conduct made a poor impression on allegedly pro-Southern Marylanders.[38]

What of the final casting up? Was Jubal's Raid a success, or did it merely waste Lee's strength to no real purpose? Fickle Richmond newspapers would soon shift from honied praise of Early to bitter vilification. From hero, he would become a scapegoat. It was in the nature of things that Southerners would condemn the raid out of bitter disappointment. High and brilliant their hopes were lifted when word came that Rebel cannon flamed against the enemy's capital, and from this Olympian height, Jubal had cast them down. He had not taken Washington; he had wasted valuable time to no understandable purpose in the lower valley; he had fought an unnecessary battle on the Monocacy; and had just missed in a race with destiny. There was the unbearable rub: he had just missed. Better to meanly lose, than just barely. Early was guilty of the worst of crimes: he was an "almost" man. To the sorely pressed Southland in 1864, there were too many of those—the list included Braxton Bragg, John Pemberton, Joseph Johnston, P. G. T. Beauregard and even Jefferson Davis. Only Lee had risen above the resources of his country, above himself and his opposition; surely the Confederacy had a right to expect that one of Lee's generals would not fail.

The main question revolves around the definition of "failure." Early failed to take Washington; he failed to win foreign recognition; he failed to draw all of Grant's army northward; he failed to lure Grant into an attack on Lee in strong works.

But what did he accomplish? He wrecked the Army of the Kanawha, and junked the careers of David Hunter and Franz Sigel; he destroyed the force of Lew Wallace at the Monocacy; he brought war deeper into the ken of Northerners than ever it had been; he laid brief siege to the enemy's capital, and drew closer to the defenses than the Federal armies yet had come to Richmond; he paralyzed the Union high command for almost two weeks and made a laughing stock of Henry Halleck; he brought from Maryland vast, invaluable stocks of horses, cattle, food and forage; he cleared the Shenandoah Valley of enemy troops at harvest time, and so fed the Army of Northern Virginia; and he shot at Abraham Lincoln. In the eyes of the world he demonstrated that the South, after four arduous years, with hostile armies near Richmond and knifing into Georgia, could still parry with one hand and thrust with the other. The power of the offensive remained.

On July 25, 1864, the London *Times* summed up the implications of the Maryland invasion: "The Confederacy is more formidable as an enemy than ever." That so splendid a ruse had been achieved is perhaps the finest tribute to Jubal's Raid.

EPILOGUE

WHAT AFTER the Raid? There was much to follow, for the Raid stood as only a phase of a larger campaign. Early's overall objective remained the same: delay enemy forces, detain them in the Shenandoah and prevent their aiding Grant at Richmond. General Lee, who had no recriminations for a Raid he rated a success, decided to leave Early in the Valley sector and enjoined him to amuse as many Federals as possible.

As a result of the Washington operations, Early's little army had considerable power of attraction and high Federal authorities were determined that he and his men should not escape severe punishment. This, of course, was just the reaction Early and Lee desired, for it meant that more Union troops would be sent to track the Army of the Valley. In August, Grant sent General Philip H. Sheridan to take charge of the pursuit and elimination of Jubal and his ragged remnants. To make Sheridan's task easier, Grant arranged that he should have about 30,000 men—mostly Union horse, but also some infantry and artillery. After some soul-searching, Grant picked Sheridan for this mission. For a time he cherished the amazing notion that David Hunter would still get into the fight and redeem his sunken reputation. But this hope faded and Grant at length concluded that some man of energy would have to recoup the fortunes of the North in the Valley area. Sheridan was an obvious choice, once Hunter disappeared from consideration. The cavalry leader had proved himself a willing and efficient fighter, had experience in commanding infantry and could be presumed to know something of the rudiments of artillery tactics. His aggressiveness matched that of Early, and this

175

put him several cuts above most Federal commanders. In the
Valley he would move swiftly, attack with devastating force,
and press forward ruthlessly. He took the assignment with
pleasure.

When news of Sheridan's assignment reached Early, he
was happy enough. He made the mistake of underestimating
this new opponent, and decided that he could play with
Sheridan at will. And for a time in August it seemed he might
be right. Skillfully, Early aimed his small force (it grew smaller
when some of his brigades were called back to Richmond) at
different parts of the lower Valley, hurled it at exposed Union
positions, fought detached units of the Federals. This game
of hit and run Early pursued with a verve and polish reminiscent of Jackson, and he made Sheridan look bad indeed. Unfortunately for Early, Sheridan took these stings with a purpose
in mind; he quietly built strength, and when he was ready he
moved to deal with the Army of the Valley. In a series of
important actions through late summer and fall Sheridan and
Early contested the Valley. At Winchester and Fisher's Hill,
Early attacked his stronger foe with his usual audacity; each
time he gained local success, but found his numbers too thin
to exploit opportunities or retrieve the day. But he stayed, and
kept on attacking with fewer and fewer men. Each attack cost
him, but each attack bought more time for Lee and forced
Sheridan to keep his large force in the Valley. On October 19,
1864, Early again hurled his army at the enemy at Cedar
Creek. His battle had been well planned, and almost total sur-
prise was achieved. The early part of the battle could be
counted as a smashing Confederate victory. At the high tide of
success, when Federals were streaming toward the rear in cha-
otic masses, Early lapsed into an old habit: uncertain of the terrain, he held up the action to see what had been done and to
take a look at the field. The delay proved fatal; Sheridan

arrived and brought reinforcements in a hairbreadth rescue, and the outcome of the battle was a shattering Rebel defeat.

Cedar Creek proved a failure the Army of the Valley could never overcome; irreplaceable men were going down in every action, and at Cedar Creek Sandie Pendleton and Dodson Ramseur fell. Early, daunted, determined nonetheless to remain in the Valley and keep harassing Sheridan. For his part Sheridan was just as glad; he concentrated strength and built his campaign to purge the Shenandoah Valley.

Winter of 1864 brought nothing but heartbreak and hardship to the Army of the Valley. Steadily Grant hammered at the Petersburg lines, and steadily Lee's ranks thinned as a result of attrition. When his lines grew too thin for safety he called on Early for help, and by the time active campaigning came to a virtual stop for the winter, Jubal's ranks had dwindled to no more than 4,000 men. These were almost an elect 4,000; they were the men who stayed when hope had gone, when rations had all but vanished, when uniforms were memories, and shoes were museum pieces; they were the hardy who had always been at the core of the army, the gaunt gray men of iron.

Sheridan opened the year 1865 with a resumption of the march up the Valley—a move in conjunction with Grant's program for a knockout offensive in the spring. Early met the advance, but this time there was no holding the bluecoats. Steadily, inexorably, they pushed the grayclads back. Finally, Early had only a corporal's guard of 1,000 left. With this shadow army he met 15,000 Federals at Waynesboro on March 31, suffered complete, utter, smashing rout—and the Army of the Valley was no more.

Defeat and degradation—these were Jubal's share of the war. The dying Confederacy heaped vilification on him for all the Shenandoah operations in 1864 and 1865, blamed him for reckless combat with vastly superior forces, accused him of throwing away his own strength, and of hopelessly incompetent generalship. His problems—inferior strength, attenuated communications, protection of vital objectives, scant resources —were, of course, not considered. All would have turned out in the South's favor had Jubal Early not been in the Valley!

This patent nonsense Jubal refused to consider. His only concern was that his beloved Confederacy was gone. In the future he would record his own estimate of his campaign and with pride: to him it ranked as a successful diversionary movement, one which could not, after the Washington phase, have done more than it did. But in detaining three times as many Federals in the Valley as there were Confederates, Jubal's mission had been accomplished. The Valley Campaign of 1864 had none of the luster of Jackson's famed operations in 1862, but things were so different that no comparison between the two could fairly be drawn. Stonewall had taught special lessons in the delicate art of maneuver and bluff, but Early was no Jackson nor was Sheridan a Banks. The Valley forces in 1864 were not the raw legions of 1862. The conclusion is inescapable: against all that was thrown at him Early conducted a sound campaign which gained the primary objective of holding Sheridan in the Shenandoah.

If Jubal cannot be rated a second Jackson, he was at least a worthy successor to Ewell and sustained the confidence placed in him by General Lee.

Early migrated from the South at war's end, traveled in Mexico, went to Canada and remained an expatriate until 1869. Probably the most thoroughly beaten of Southern generals, he remained the most thoroughly unreconstructed of Rebels. Nursing his disappointment, his hatred of the victors, he returned finally to Virginia, but soon allied himself with General P. G. T. Beauregard in managing the lucrative Louisiana Lottery. This provided financial ease, and he spent the remaining years of his life writing on various aspects of the war.

In 1866 he had published a bitter diatribe entitled *A Memoir of the Last Year of the War for Independence in the Confederate States of America,* a vindictive book bristling with untempered judgments. But he also began compiling his memoirs, and as he wrote and rewrote these, the fire of frustration cooled. When the book was published in 1912—eighteen years after his death in 1894—it gained admiration as a dispassionate, careful book which was valuable as a tool for history. In a way his *Autobiographical Sketch and Narrative* stands as Early's best literary achievement, for it shows that underneath the stormy exterior he was a man of reason and sense.

He deserves an honored place in the ranks of Confederate generals. A good administrator—with some lapses concerning the mounted arm—he was a natural leader, a quick and generally sound tactician, a good strategist. His campaign in the Valley in 1864 did more than most diversions to form a pattern in war; what he did in the Shenandoah certainly prolonged the conflict through the winter of 1864, and, had he been able to brush past the militia at Washington's battlements, he might have altered the course of history.

NOTES

CHAPTER 1   *Troubles Comes in Threes*

1. *Richmond Sentinel,* June 21, 1864; *War of the Rebellion: A Compilation of the Official Records of the Union and Confederate Armies* (70 vols. in 127 and index; Washington, 1880–1901. Cited hereinafter as *OR*), ser. I, vol. 37, pt. 1, p. 96.
2. Douglas Southall Freeman, *R. E. Lee: A Biography* (4 vols.; New York, 1934–1935), III, p. 397.
3. *Ibid.,* pp. 397–398.   4. *OR,* I, 37, pt. 1, pp. 150–151.
5. Douglas Southall Freeman (ed.), *Lee's Dispatches: Unpublished Letters of General Robert E. Lee, C.S.A. to Jefferson Davis and the War Department of The Confederate States of America, 1862–65* (New York, 1915), p. 218.
6. Freeman, *Lee,* III, p. 396; Freeman (ed.), *Lee's Dispatches,* p. 217.
7. Freeman, *Lee,* III, p. 397.
8. See the comprehensive railroad map in Robert C. Black, III, *The Railroads of the Confederacy* (Chapel Hill, 1952); *OR,* I, 36, pt. 1, pp. 1034, 1095: Douglas Southall Freeman, *Lee's Lieutenants: A Study in Command* (3 vols.; New York, 1942–1944), III, p. 516.
9. Freeman, *Lee's Lieutenants,* III, p. 517.   10. *Ibid.,* p. 518.
11. See *OR,* I, 36, pt. 1, pp. 796–797, where Sheridan's reasons for retreating are obviously absurd. The reasons given by his subordinate, Gen. A. T. A. Torbert, are more realistic. See *ibid.,* p. 809, and Freeman, *Lee's Lieutenants,* III, p. 522.
12. Freeman, *Lee,* III, p. 401.
13. John S. Wise, *The End of an Era* (Boston, 1899), p. 310.
14. *Ibid.*   15. *Ibid.,* p. 311.   16. *Ibid.,* p. 312.
17. Col. William Couper, *One Hundred Years at V.M.I.* (4 vols.; Richmond, Va., 1939), III, p. 35.
18. *OR,* I, 37, pt. 1, pp. 97–98.
19. See the penetrating summary of the difficult tactical situation in Freeman, *Lee,* III, chap. 23.
20. See [Jed. Hotchkiss] MS Report of Engineering Operations of the Army of the Valley District, dated March 2, 1865, in the Jubal A. Early Papers, Library of Congress, Washington, D.C. (Microfilm copies of the Early Papers are in the Fondren Library, The William Marsh Rice University.) The date of Early's assumption of command is given as June 5, 1864.

21. Jubal Anderson Early, *A Memoir of the Last Year of the War for Independence in the Confederate States of America*. . . . (Lynchburg, Va., 1867. Cited hereinafter as Early, *Last Year*), p. 40; Early, *Autobiographical Sketch and Narrative of the War Between the States* (with notes by R. H. Early. Philadelphia, 1912. Cited hereinafter as *Early*), p. 371.

CHAPTER 2   *Hunter Hunted*

1. *Early*, p. 371; Early, *Last Year*, p. 40.
2. The order has not been found, but its contents may be inferred from Early's remarks in *Early*, p. 371, and in Early, *Last Year*, p. 40, and in *OR*, I, 37, pt. 1, p. 767.
3. MS Journal of Jedediah Hotchkiss, Monday, June 13, 1864. The typescript of Hotchkiss' Journal is in the Hotchkiss Papers, Manuscripts Division, Library of Congress, Washington, D.C. A microfilm copy is in the possession of the author. Cited hereinafter as Hotchkiss Journ.
4. Hotchkiss Journ., June 13, 1864.
5. Freeman, *Lee's Lieutenants*, III, p. 391; John B. Gordon, *Reminiscences of the Civil War* (New York, 1903), pp. 258–261.
6. Freeman, *Lee's Lieutenants*, III, p. 448.   7. Quoted in *ibid.*, p. 511.
8. Ezra J. Warner, *Generals in Gray* (Baton Rouge, La., 1959), pp. 191–192; A. L. Long, *Memoirs of Robert E. Lee* (New York, 1886), pp. 355–356.
9. *OR*, I, 36, pt. 1, p. 1047.   10. *Ibid.*, 37, pt. 1, p. 753.
11. *Ibid.*, pp. 755–761.   12. Hotchkiss Journ., June 14, 1864.
13. *OR*, I, 51, pt. 2, pp. 1012–1013.
14. Hotchkiss Journ., June 14, 15, 1864.
15. *OR*, I, 37, pt. 1, p. 761.   16. Hotchkiss Journ., June 15, 1864.
17. *Ibid.; Early*, pp. 372–373.   18. *OR*, I, 37, pt. 1, p. 763.
19. Hotchkiss Journ., June 16, 1864; [Jed. Hotchkiss] MS Report of Engineering Operations of the Army of the Valley, p. 9; *OR*, I, 37, pt. 1, p. 763.
20. *OR*, I, 37, pt. 1, p. 763.   21. *Ibid.*, pp. 98–150.
22. *Ibid.*, p. 99.   23. Hotchkiss Journ., June 17, 1864.
24. Charles M. Blackford, "The Campaign and Battle of Lynchburg," in *Southern Historical Society Papers* (Richmond, Va.), (1902), p. 288; *Early*, p. 373; Gordon, *Reminiscences*, p. 300; MS Diary of Capt. W. W. Old, Aide-de-Camp to General Early, June 17, 1864. Typescript copy of the diary is in the Jubal A. Early Papers, Library of Congress, vol. 3–5.
25. *Early*, 373.
26. The timing is based on the average speed of twenty-five miles an hour with a little extra allowance. This rate was not unknown to Confederate railroads. See Black, *Railroads of the Confederacy*, pp. 31–32.

27. Freeman, *Lee's Lieutenants*, II, p. 526; *Early*, p. 373; Early, *Last Year*, pp. 42–43.
28. Freeman, *Lee's Lieutenants*, III, p. 526; *OR*, I, 51, pt. 2, p. 1020.
29. *Early*, p. 374; Blackford, "Campaign and Battle of Lynchburg," *Southern Historical Society Papers*, XXX, p. 288; Freeman, *Lee's Lieutenants*, III, p. 527.
30. *OR*, I, 37, pt. 1, p. 127.
31. *Ibid.*, pp. 99, 121, 126, 127, 128, 130, 147, 148; MS Diary of Capt. W. W. Old, June 17, 1864.
32. Early, *Last Year*, p. 43; Blackford, "Campaign and Battle of Lynchburg," in *Southern Historical Society Papers*, XXX, p. 288–289.
33. *OR*, I, 37, pt. 1, p. 141.
34. This is a rough approximation, based on Hunter's known strength of about 18,000 and the estimate made by Capt. C. M. Blackford that when all of Early's infantry were in line, the Confederates numbered a little more than half of the Federal strength. See *Southern Historical Society Papers*, XXX, p. 290.
35. Special Orders Number 141, Adjutant and Inspector General's Office, Richmond, June 17, 1864; *OR*, I, 37, pt. 1, p. 765. The same order is in *ibid.*, 40, pt. 2, p. 662.
36. *OR*, I, 37, pt. 1, p. 147.
37. For Ransom's assignment to command, see *OR*, I, 40, pt. 2, pp. 645–646. For Breckinridge's condemnation of Imboden, see *ibid.*, p. 658, and *ibid.*, 37, pt. 1, p. 762.
38. *Early*, p. 375; Early, *Last Year*, p. 44; Blackford, "Campaign and Battle of Lynchburg," *Southern Historical Society Papers*, XXX, p. 291.
39. Hotchkiss Journ., June 18, 1864.
40. *Daily National Intelligencer* (Washington, D. C.), July 4, 1864. Quoting the Richmond *Enquirer*, June 24, 1864.
41. Early, *Last Year*, p. 44, *Early*, p. 375; Blackford, "Campaign and Battle of Lynchburg," in *Southern Historical Society Papers*, XXX, p. 290.
42. *OR*, I, 37, pt. 1, pp. 99, 121, 130, 132, 141–142, 148.
43. *Ibid.*, p. 141.   44. *Ibid.*, pp. 141, 649.   45. *Ibid.*, p. 142.
46. *Ibid.*, p. 650.   47. *Ibid.*, pp. 142–143.
48. Probably at 9 A.M. See *ibid.*, p. 132.
49. For examples of Federal lethargy on the Confederate left, see *ibid.*, pp. 100, 121, 130; see also Blackford, "Campaign and Battle of Lynchburg," in *Southern Historical Society Papers*, XXX, p. 291.
50. *OR*, I, 37, pt. 1, p. 766.   51. Wise, *End of an Era*, pp. 313–314.
52. *OR*, I, 37, pt. 1, pp. 100, 121, 130, 133, 135, 142–143, 148.
53. Early, *Last Year*, pp. 44–45.   54. Hotchkiss Journ., June 19, 1864.
55. *OR*, I, 37, pt. 1, p. 160.   56. *Ibid.*, pp. 121, 148.
57. MS Diary of Capt. W. W. Old, June 19, 1864.
58. Early, *Last Year*, p. 45.
59. *Early*, p. 377; Hotchkiss Journ., June 20, 1864.

60. Early, *Last Year*, p. 46; Hotchkiss Journ., June 21, 1864; MS Diary of Capt. W. W. Old, June 21, 1864.
61. MS Diary of Capt. W. W. Old, June 21, 1864.
62. John H. Worsham, *One of Jackson's Foot Cavalry* (New York, 1912. Cited hereinafter as *Worsham*), p. 230.
63. [Jed. Hotchkiss] MS Report of Engineering Operations of the Army of the Valley, p. 11; Clement A. Evans (ed.), *Confederate Military History* (12 vols. and supp. vol.; Atlanta, Ga., 1899), III, p. 478.
64. *OR*, I, 37, pt. 1, pp. 101–102.

CHAPTER 3   *Into the Valley*

1. Henry Kyd Douglas, *I Rode With Stonewall* (Chapel Hill, 1940), p. 291.
2. Freeman (ed.), *Lee's Dispatches*, p. 241.
3. John O. Casler, *Four Years in the Stonewall Brigade* (Girard, Kans., 1906; reprint edition, Marietta, Ga., 1951), pp. 227, 228, 229–230.
4. Hotchkiss Journ., June 23, 1864; *OR*, I, 37, pt. 1, pp. 766–767; *Early*, p. 380; Early, *Last Year*, p. 48.
5. Hotchkiss Journ., June 23, 1864.
6. *Ibid.*, June 24, 1864; MS Diary of Capt. W. W. Old, June 24, 1864.
7. Douglas, *I Rode With Stonewall*, p. 291.
8. Douglas, *I Rode With Stonewall*, p. 291. The quotation is a variant of Tennyson's *Maude*, I, xxii, 69–71. See also MS Diary of Capt. W. W. Old, June 25, 1864; *Worsham*, p. 231; W. G. Bean, *Stonewall's Man: Sandie Pendleton* (Chapel Hill, 1959), p. 205; Freeman, *Lee's Lieutenants*, III, p. 557.
9. *Early*, p. 381.   10. *Ibid.*
11. For descriptions of the condition of the harvest see the Richmond *Sentinel*, June 29, 1864, quoting the Lynchburg *Republican* and the Rockingham *Register;* also the *Sentinel*, July 4, 1864; *Daily National Intelligencer*, June 18, July 4, 1864, quoting Cincinnati *Gazette*.
12. *OR*, I, 51, pt. 2, pp. 1028–1029.   13. *Worsham*, p. 231.
14. Casler, *Four Years in the Stonewall Brigade*, p. 227.
15. Long, *Memoirs of Robert E. Lee*, pp. 355–356.
16. Freeman, *Lee's Lieutenants*, III, p. 558; Warner, *Generals in Gray*, pp. 347–348.
17. Freeman, *Lee's Lieutenants*, III, p. 558; Allen P. Tankersley, *John B. Gordon: A Study in Gallantry* (Atlanta, Ga., 1955), p. 156.
18. Gordon, *Reminiscences*, pp. 317–318.
19. Freeman, *Lee's Lieutenants*, III, p. 578.
20. *Ibid.*, pp. xxiv, xl; Gordon, *Reminiscences*, pp. 63–64.
21. See Freeman, *Lee's Lieutenants*, II, pp. xv, 325–327.
22. *OR*, I, 40, pt. 2, p. 658.
23. *Ibid.*, 37, pt. 1, p. 768; *Early*, p. 381; Early, *Last Year*, p. 49.

24. Jennings C. Wise, *The Long Arm of Lee* (2 vols.; Lynchburg, Va., 1915), II, p. 877.

25. *Ibid.*   26. *OR*, I, 37, pt. 1, p. 768.

27. *Ibid.; ibid.*, 51, pt. 2, pp. 1028–1029.

28. *OR*, I, 37, pt. 1, pp. 766–767.

29. Early's letter has not been found, but its contents may be conjectured from Lee to Jefferson Davis, Petersburg, June 29, 1864, in *OR*, I, 37, pt. 1, pp. 769–770.

30. For numbers see Freeman, *Lee's Lieutenants*, III, p. 558.

31. MS Diary of Capt. W. W. Old, June 28, 1864.

32. *Ibid.*, June 30, 1864; [Jed. Hotchkiss] MS Report of Engineering Operations of the Army of the Valley, p. 12.

33. MD Diary of Capt. W. W. Old, June 30, 1864; [Jed. Hotchkiss] MS Report of Engineering Operations of the Army of the Valley, p. 12.

34. *OR*, I, 51, pt. 2, pp. 1028–1029.   35. Hotchkiss Journ., July 2, 1864.

36. Early, *Last Year*, pp. 50–51; *Early*, p. 383. For Lee's continuing approval of Early's program, see *OR*, I, 37, pt. 1, pp. 769–770.

37. Hotchkiss Journ., July 3, 1864.

38. *OR*, I, 37, pt. 1, pp. 175–176; Early, *Last Year*, p. 51.

39. *Ibid.*, p. 185.

40. *Ibid.*, pp. 175–176; Early, *Last Year*, p. 51; Hotchkiss Journ., July 3, 1864; MS Diary of Capt. W. W. Old, July 3, 1864.

41. *OR*, I, 37, pt. 1, pp. 766–767.   42. *Worsham*, pp. 232–233.

43. *Ibid.*, p. 233.

44. Hotchkiss Journ., July 4, 1863; MS Diary of Capt. W. W. Old, July 4, 1864.

45. Douglas, *I Rode With Stonewall*, p. 292.

46. *OR*, I, 37, pt. 1, pp. 185–186.

47. *Ibid.*, p. 4; [Jed. Hotchkiss] MS Report of Engineering Operations of the Army of the Valley, p. 13.

48. *OR*, I, 37, pt. 2, p. 592.   49. *Worsham*, pp. 233–234.

50. Hotchkiss Journ., July 5, 1864; *OR*, I, 37, pt. 2, pp. 591, 592.

51. Hotchkiss Journ., July 5, 6, 1864.

52. Douglas, *I Rode With Stonewall*, p. 293.

CHAPTER 4   *Fateful Hours on a River*

1. Douglas, *I Rode With Stonewall*, p. 293.

2. The order was issued July 5. See *OR*, I, 37, pt. 2, p. 592.

3. Early, *Last Year*, p. 53; *Early*, p. 386.

4. Millard K. Bushong, *Old Jube: A Biography of General Jubal A. Early* (Boyce, Va., 1955), p. 197; *Early*, p. 385.

5. Robert E. Lee, Jr., *Recollections and Letters of General Robert E. Lee* (New York, 1904), p. 131.

6. *OR*, I, 37, pt. 1, pp. 769–770.　　　7. Hotchkiss Journ., July 7, 1864.
8. Lew Wallace, *Autobiography* (2 vols.; New York, 1906), II, pp. 715, 717.
9. *Ibid.*, pp. 721–723.　　　10. *Ibid.*, pp. 721–730.
11. *Worsham*, p. 235; Wallace, *Autobiography*, II, p. 713.
12. Bradley T. Johnson, "My Ride Around Baltimore in Eighteen Hundred and Sixty-Four," in *Southern Historical Society Papers*, XXX (1902. Cited hereinafter as Johnson, "My Ride"), p. 217; Wallace, *Autobiography*, II, pp. 729–731.
13. See Wallace, *Autobiography*, II, p. 731.　　　14. *Ibid.*, p. 725.
15. *Daily National Intelligencer*, July 7, 1864.
16. Wallace, *Autobiography*, II, p. 726.
17. *Ibid.*, pp. 710–711.　　　18. *Ibid.*, p. 725.　　　19. *Ibid.*, p. 731.
20. General Lewis followed with supplies captured at Harpers Ferry. See *Early*, p. 386.
21. Hotchkiss Journal, July 8, 1864.
22. Johnson, "My Ride," pp. 217–218.
23. *Worsham*, p. 235; *OR*, I, 37, pt. 1, p. 196; Freeman, *Lee's Lieutenants*, III, pp. 560–562.
24. Bushong, *Old Jube*, p. 197; Bean, *Stonewall's Man*, p. 205. Payment was made late in the day after word of the outcome of fighting at the Monocacy convinced the city fathers that no help would reach them from Wallace. The money came from Frederick's five banks, and the city assumed the debt in later years after fruitless attempts to get Federal compensation. The last payment on the debt was made in October, 1951. In April, 1960, renewed efforts were made in the United States Congress to obtain Federal indemnity. (Bushong, *Old Jube*, p. 197; Houston (Texas) *Press*, April 27, 1960.)
25. R. U. Johnson and C. C. Buel (eds.), *Battles and Leaders of the Civil War* (4 vols.; New York, 1887–1888; reprint edition, New York, 1956), IV, p. 499. The figure given in the text is an attempt to reconcile several estimates.
26. Freeman, *Lee's Lieutenants*, III, p. 560; Frank Moore (ed.), *The Rebellion* (12 vols.; New York, 1862–1871), XI, pp. 615–616; *OR*, I, 37, pt. 1, p. 96.
27. *Worsham*, p. 236.　　　28. *OR*, I, 37, pt. 1, p. 350.
29. Wallace, *Autobiography*, II, p. 752.
30. *Ibid.*, pp. 758–766; Moore, *Rebellion Record*, XI, pp. 615–616.
31. *OR*, I, 37, pt. 1, p. 352.　　　32. *Ibid.*, p. 204.
33. *Worsham*, p. 239.
34. Douglas, *I Rode With Stonewall*, p. 293; Hotchkiss Journ., July 9, 1864; Bean, *Stonewall's Man*, p. 206; *Early*, p. 388.
35. *Worsham*, p. 240.
36. *OR*, I, 37, pt. 1, pp. 201–202, 348.
37. Douglas, *I Rode With Stonewall*, p. 294; MS Diary of Capt. W. W. Old, July 10, 1864. The difference between these two accounts is amusing.

Douglas served with the rear guard, but wrote of it much later. Old recounted the day's events with typical neutrality.

38. Hotchkiss Journ., July 10, 1864; MS Diary of Capt. W. W. Old, July 10, 1864.
39. Hotchkiss Journ., July 10, 1864.
40. *OR,* I, 37, pt. 2, pp. 193, 166–167.

CHAPTER 5   *Let Us Be Vigilant*

1. See J. G. Barnard, *A Report on the Defenses of Washington* (Washington, 1871).
2. See T. Harry Williams, *Lincoln Finds a General* (New York, 1952; reprint edition, New York, 1956). Studies of Lincoln are, of course, legion. See especially Carl Sandburg, *Abraham Lincoln: The War Years* (4 vols.; New York, 1945); Lord Charnwood, *Abraham Lincoln* (New York, 1917); Benjamin P. Thomas, *Abraham Lincoln,* (New York, 1953).
3. For much of the material on the internal situation in Washington, see the splendid chapter in Margaret Leech, *Reveille in Washington* (New York, 1941), entitled "Siege in the Suburbs" (pp. 329–346). See also *Daily National Intelligencer,* June 30, July 4, 1864.
4. [Lucius E. Chittenden], "Washington Experiences," MS account in the author's possession. See also Chittenden, *Recollections of President Lincoln and His Administration* (New York, 1891), pp. 385–427.
5. *OR,* I, 37, pt. 2, pp. 34–35.   6. *Ibid.,* pp. 33–34.
7. *Ibid.,* pp. 57–58.   8. *Ibid.,* pp. 58–59.   9. *Ibid.,* pp. 67–68.
10. *Ibid.,* p. 15.   11. *Ibid.,* p. 98.   12. *Ibid.,* pp. 104, 81, 63.
13. *Ibid.,* p. 91.   14. *Ibid.,* p. 62.
15. *Daily National Intelligencer,* July 7–11, 1864, quoting Baltimore dispatches.
16. Gideon Welles, *Diary* (3 vols.; Boston, 1911), II, p. 70.
17. Glenn H. Worthington, *Fighting For Time; or, The Battle That Saved Washington and Mayhap the Union* (Frederick, Md. [printed in Baltimore], 1932), pp. 182–183.
18. William V. Cox, "The Defenses of Washington—General Early's Advance on the Capital and the Battle of Fort Stevens, July 11 and 12, 1864," in *Records of the Columbia Historical Society,* IV (1901), p. 142.
19. *OR,* I, 37, pt. 2, pp. 136, 195.   20. *Ibid.,* p. 236.
21. *Ibid.,* pp. 224, 225.   22. *Ibid.,* pp. 81, 162.
23. *Ibid.,* pp. 83–85.   24. *Ibid.,* pp. 166–167.
25. *Ibid.,* pp. 140, 173.

CHAPTER 6   *Rebels at the Ramparts*

1. *OR*, I, 37, pt. 2, p. 594.
2. Early, *Last Year*, p. 56; *Worsham*, pp. 241–242.
3. *Worsham*, pp. 241–242.
4. Early, *Last Year*, pp. 56–57; MS Diary of Capt. W. W. Old, July 11, 1864; Hotchkiss Journ., July 11, 1864.
5. *OR*, I, 37, pt. 2, p. 209.   6. *Worsham*, p. 241.
7. Early, *Last Year*, p. 58.   8. Hotchkiss Journ., July 11, 1864.
9. Early, *Last Year*, pp. 58–59.
10. Leech, *Reveille in Washington*, p. 345; Douglas, *I Rode With Stonewall*, pp. 294–295.
11. See Gordon, *Reminiscences*, pp. 314–315; Freeman, *Lee's Lieutenants*, III, p. 566; Early, *Last Year*, p. 59; *OR*, I, 37, pt. 1, p. 348.
12. Early, *Last Year*, p. 59.   13. Johnson, "My Ride," pp. 218–219.
14. Early, *Last Year*, p. 59.   15. *OR*, I, 37, pt. 2, pp. 203, 199.
16. *Ibid.*, p. 155.   17. *Ibid.*, pt. 1, pp. 254–260.   18. *Ibid.*, p. 273.
19. *Ibid.*, pt. 2, p. 209.   20. Leech, *Reveille in Washington*, p. 339.
21. *OR*, I, 37, pt. 2, p. 208.   22 Welles, *Diary*, II, p. 72.
23. *Frank Leslie's Illustrated Newspaper* (New York), August 13, 1864, p. 324.
24. [Lucius E. Chittenden], "A Chapter for My Children to Read," [pp. 4–5]. MS in author's possession.
25. *Frank Leslie's Illustrated Newspaper*, July 30, 1864, p. 290.
26. *OR*, I, 37, pt. 1, p. 270.   27. Johnson, "My Ride," p. 222.
28. William B. Conway, "Talks With General J. A. Early," in *Southern Historical Society* Papers, XXX (1902), p. 255.
29. [Lucius E. Chittenden], "A Chapter for My Children to Read," [pp. 5–6].
30. See John H. Cramer, *Lincoln Under Enemy Fire* (Baton Rouge, La., 1948), *passim;* Leech, *Reveille in Washington*, p. 343; Thomas W. Hyde, *Following the Greek Cross* (Boston, 1894), p. 223; Bushong, *Old Jube*, p. 208.
31. The timing here is difficult to establish with certainty. Welles, *Diary*, II, p. 75, is authority for the fact that Lincoln was not on the parapet at the time action opened.
32. [Lucius E. Chittenden], "A Chapter for My Children to Read," [pp. 8–9].
33. See Wheaton's figures in *OR*, I, 37, pt. 1, p. 277.
34. Douglas, *I Rode With Stonewall*, p. 295; *OR*, I, 37, pt. 1, p. 232.
35. Johnson rejoined after midnight with his command relatively intact. See Johnson, "My Ride," p. 222.
36. Douglas, *I Rode With Stonewall*, p. 296.
37. Johnson, "My Ride," p. 222.   38. *Ibid.*, p. 219.

BIBLIOGRAPHY

MANUSCRIPTS

Lucius E. Chittenden Manuscript Notes on Washington, D.C. A valuable collection of memoranda compiled by Lincoln's Register of the Treasury. Chittenden wrote a good deal about his experiences in the government during the Civil War, and this manuscript volume apparently served as rough notes for some of his later books. The manuscript is in the author's private possession.

Jubal Anderson Early Papers. An extensive and excellent collection of material relating to the life of General Early. The collection is in the Manuscripts Division, Library of Congress. A microfilm copy of the Early Papers is in the Fondren Library, Rice University, Houston, Texas.

Diary and Journal of Major Jedediah Hotchkiss. An invaluable journal kept by a perceptive diarist who served on the staff of General Stonewall Jackson, then on the staff of General Richard Ewell, and finally on the staff of General Early. The Journal is in the extensive Hotchkiss collection, Manuscripts Division, Library of Congress. A microfilm copy of the Journal is in the Fondren Library, Rice University.

Jedediah Hotchkiss, "Report of Engineering Operations of the Army of the Valley District," March 2, 1865. A copy of this report is in the J. A. Early Papers, Manuscripts Division, Library of Congress.

Diary of Captain W. W. Old, Aide-de-Camp to General Early, kept from June 13, 1864 to August 12, 1864. In the J. A. Early Papers, Library of Congress.

NEWSPAPERS

Daily National Intelligencer (Washington, D.C.), June–July, 1864.
Frank Leslie's Illustrated Newspaper (New York), July–August, 1864.
Richmond Enquirer (Richmond, Va.; semiweekly edition), June–July, 1864.
Richmond Sentinel (Richmond, Va.), June–July, 1864.

PRINTED SOURCES AND SECONDARY WORKS

Agassiz, George R. (ed.). *Meade's Headquarters, 1863–1865: Letters of Colonel Theodore Lyman from the Wilderness to Appomattox.* Boston, 1922.

Alexander, Edward P. *Military Memoirs of a Confederate.* New York, 1910.

Barnard, J. G. *A Report on the Defenses of Washington.* Washington, D.C., 1871.

Bean, W. G. *Stonewall's Man: Sandie Pendleton.* Chapel Hill, 1959.

Black, Robert C., III. *The Railroads of the Confederacy.* Chapel Hill, 1952.

Blackford, Captain Charles M. "The Campaign and Battle of Lynchburg," *Southern Historical Society Papers,* XXX (1902), 279–332.

Bowen, Katherine D. *Yankee from Olympus.* New York, 1944.

Bradwell, J. G. "First Valley Campaign of General Early," *Confederate Veteran,* XIX (1911), 230–231.

———. "Early's Demonstration Against Washington in 1864," *Confederate Veteran,* XXII (1914), 438–439.

———. "Early's March to Washington in 1864," *Confederate Veteran,* XXVIII (1920), 176–177.

———. "Cold Harbor, Lynchburg, Valley Campaign, etc., 1864," *Confederate Veteran,* XXVIII (1920), 138–139.

[Brock, Sally] A Richmond Lady. *Richmond During the War.* New York, 1867.

Burne, Alfred H. *Lee, Grant and Sherman.* Aldershot, England, 1938.

———. "Early's Valley Campaign," *Fighting Forces,* XVI (1939–40), 236–246.

Bushong, Millard K. *Old Jube: A Biography of General Jubal A. Early.* Boyce, Va., 1955.

Casler, John O. *Four Years in the Stonewall Brigade.* Girard, Kans., 1906. Reprint edition, Marietta, Ga., 1951.

Chase, Salmon P. *Inside Lincoln's Cabinet; Civil War Diaries.* (Edited by David Donald.) New York, 1954.

Conway, William B. "Talks With General J. A. Early," *Southern Historical Society Papers,* XXX (1902), 250–255.

Couper, Colonel William. *One Hundred Years at V.M.I.* 4 vols. Richmond, 1939.

Cox, William V. "The Defenses of Washington—General Early's Advance on the Capital and the Battle of Fort Stevens, July 11 and 12, 1864," *Records of the Columbia Historical Society,* IV (1901), 135–165.

Cramer, John Henry. *Lincoln Under Enemy Fire.* Baton Rouge, La., 1948.

Dana, Charles A. *Recollections of the Civil War.* New York, 1898.

Davis, Jefferson. *Rise and Fall of the Confederate Government.* 2 vols. New York, 1881.

Douglas, Henry Kyd. *I Rode With Stonewall.* Chapel Hill, 1940.

Early, Jubal A. *A Memoir of the Last Year of the War for Independence, in the Confederate States of America.* Lynchburg, Va., 1867.

———. *Autobiographical Sketch and Narrative of the War Between the States.* (Edited by R. H. Early.) Philadelphia, 1912.

———. "The Advance on Washington in 1864," *Southern Historical Society Papers,* IX (1881), 297–312.

Early, Jubal A. *Report, and Addresses in Relation to the War Between the States*. [n. p., n. d.]

Evans, Clement A. (ed.). *Confederate Military History*. 12 vols. Atlanta, 1899.

Freeman, Douglas Southall (ed.). *Lee's Dispatches: Unpublished Letters of General Robert E. Lee, C. S. A., to Jefferson Davis and the War Department of the Confederate States of America, 1862–65*. New York, 1915.

———. *Lee's Lieutenants: A Study in Command*. 3 vols. New York, 1942–1944.

———. *R. E. Lee: A Biography*. 4 vols. New York, 1934–1935.

Fuller, J. F. C. *Grant and Lee: A Study in Personality and Generalship*. London, 1933.

Gordon, John B. *Reminiscences of the Civil War*. New York, 1903.

Gorham, George C. *Life and Public Services of Edwin M. Stanton*. 2 vols. Boston, 1899.

Grant, U. S. *Personal Memoirs*. 2 vols. New York, 1886.

Hendrick, J. B. *Lincoln's War Cabinet*. New York, 1946.

Hesseltine, W. B. *Lincoln and the War Governors*. New York, 1948.

Howe, Mark De Wolfe (ed.). *Touched With Fire: Civil War Letters and Diary of Oliver Wendell Holmes, Jr*. Cambridge, Mass., 1947.

Humphreys, Andrew A. *The Virginia Campaign of '64 and '65*. New York, 1908.

Hyde, Thomas W. *Following the Greek Cross: or, Memories of the Sixth Army Corps*. Boston, 1894.

Johnson, Bradley T. "My Ride Around Baltimore in Eighteen Hundred and Sixty-Four," *Southern Historical Society Papers*, XXX (1892), 215–225.

Johnson, R. U., and C. C. Buel (eds.). *Battles and Leaders of the Civil War*. 4 vols. New York, 1887–1888. Reprint edition, 1956.

Jones, J. William. *Life and Letters of Robert Edward Lee, Soldier and Man*. New York, 1906.

Lee, Captain Robert E. *Recollections and Letters of General Robert E. Lee*. New York, 1904.

Leech, Margaret. *Reveille in Washington, 1860–1865*. New York, 1941.

Long, A. L. *Memoirs of Robert E. Lee*. New York, 1886.

Lounsbury, T. R. "In the Defenses of Wshington," *Yale Review*, NS II (1913), 385–411.

McKee, Irving. *"Ben-Hur" Wallace: The Life of General Lew Wallace*. Berkeley, Calif., 1947.

McKim, Randolph H. *A Soldier's Recollections*. New York, 1910.

Moore, Frank (ed.). *The Rebellion Record*. 12 vols. New York, 1862–1871.

Plum, William R. *The Military Telegraph During the Civil War in the United States*. 2 vols. Chicago, 1882.

Rowland, Dunbar (ed.). *Jefferson Davis, Constitutionalist: His Letters, Papers and Speeches*. 10 vols. Jackson, Miss., 1923.

Sorrel, G. Moxley. *Recollections of a Confederate Staff Officer*. (Reprint edition edited by B. I. Wiley.) Jackson, Tenn., 1958.

Stark, W. B. "Great Skedaddle; General Hunter's Retreat from Lynchburg," *Atlantic*, CLXII (1938), 86–94.

Tankersley, Allen P. *John B. Gordon: A Study in Gallantry*. Atlanta, 1955.

Taylor, B. F. *Pictures of Life in Camp and Field*. Chicago, 1875.

Thomas, Benjamin P. *Abraham Lincoln*. New York, 1952.

——. (ed.). *Three Years With Grant as Recalled by War Correspondent Sylvanus Cadwallader*. New York, 1955.

Thomas, Henry W. *A History of the Doles-Cook Brigade, Army of Northern Virginia, C. S. A.* Atlanta, 1903.

Townsend, George A. *Rustics in Rebellion*. Chapel Hill, 1950.

Vandiver, Frank E. (ed.). *Civil War Diary of General Josiah Gorgas*. University, Ala., 1947.

——. *Mighty Stonewall*. New York, 1957.

Wallace, Lew. *Autobiography*. 2 vols. New York, 1906.

War of the Rebellion: A Compilation of the Official Records of the Union and Confederate Armies. 70 vols. in 127 and index. Washington, D. C., 1880–1901.

Warner, Ezra J. *Generals in Gray: Lives of the Confederate Commanders*. Baton Rouge, La., 1959.

Welles, Gideon. *Diary*. 3 vols. Boston, 1909–1911.

Williams, T. Harry. *Lincoln and His Generals*. New York, 1952.

Wise, Jennings C. *The Long Arm of Lee*. 2 vols. Lynchburg, Va., 1915.

Wise, John S. *The End of an Era*. Boston, 1899.

Woollcott, Alexander. "Get Down You Fool! Early's Raid and Meeting of Lincoln and Holmes," *Atlantic*, CLXI (1938), 169–173.

Worsham, John H. *One of Jackson's Foot Cavalry*. New York, 1912.

Worthington, Glenn H. *Fighting for Time; or the Battle that Saved Washington ad Mayhap the Union*. Frederick, Md. [Printed in Baltimore], 1932.

Younger, Edward (ed.). *Inside the Confederate Government: The Diary of Robert Garlick Hill Kean*. New York, 1957.

INDEX